ASPECTS OF
MODERN CHURCH HISTORY
1517–2017
FROM AN AFRICAN PERSPECTIVE

Malcolm McCall

WESTBOW
PRESS®
A DIVISION OF THOMAS NELSON
& ZONDERVAN

WestBow Press books may be ordered through booksellers or by contacting:

WestBow Press
A Division of Thomas Nelson & Zondervan
1663 Liberty Drive
Bloomington, IN 47403
www.westbowpress.com
1 (866) 928-1240

Because of the dynamic nature of the Internet, any web addresses or links contained in
this book may have changed since publication and may no longer be valid. The views
expressed in this work are solely those of the author and do not necessarily reflect the
views of the publisher, and the publisher hereby disclaims any responsibility for them.

Any people depicted in stock imagery provided by Getty Images are models,
and such images are being used for illustrative purposes only.
Certain stock imagery © Getty Images.

Scripture quotations marked (NIV) are taken from the Holy Bible, New
International Version®, NIV®. Copyright © 1973, 1978, 1984, 2011 by Biblica,
Inc.™ Used by permission of Zondervan. All rights reserved worldwide. www.
zondervan.com The "NIV" and "New International Version" are trademarks
registered in the United States Patent and Trademark Office by Biblica, Inc.™

Scripture quotations marked NRSV are taken from the New Revised
Standard Version of the Bible, Copyright © 1989, by the Division of
Christian Education of the National Council of the Churches of Christ in
the United States of America. Used by permission. All rights reserved.

Scripture taken from the King James Version of the Bible.

ISBN: 978-1-9736-2407-3 (sc)
ISBN: 978-1-9736-2406-6 (e)

Print information available on the last page.

WestBow Press rev. date: 04/20/2018

To
the praise of God's Glory,
for the hastening of His Kingdom's coming
and
for our vibrant young African students,
as they prepare for leadership in the Church.

CONTENTS

ACKNOWLEDGEMENTS

The privilege of exploring the issues raised in this book represents, for me, a lifetime's journey, most of it shared with my precious wife Janet. We first met as young teachers in Kailahun Methodist Secondary School, up-country in Sierra Leone, in the 1960s. During those early years, she taught me so much about what it means to live a Christ-centred life. She has been my closest friend and best human guide ever since. We were engaged to be married just before we left Sierra Leone in 1970, and returned to the Kailahun area for my doctoral research when our elder daughter, Joy, was only six months old. Our younger daughter, Danielle, in 2000 married a wonderful Capetonian, David; and we are very proud of our three African grandchildren. Daughters Joy and Danielle, with her husband David, have been such blessing and encouragement in the production of this volume. In particular, David has put at our disposal his professional IT skills.

As the book-project developed, Janet has been my heart-companion at every stage, sharing in the personal journey of discovery, reformation and renewal, which has been at its core. She has shared in every dimension: from its lecture-form in the Methodist University of Kenya, to transforming it into a book. Then, as the writing progressed, she has painstakingly edited and proof-read it over and again. She is really the co-author of this book! Only God knows the depth of gratitude in my heart for her, at every level.

The Revd Dr Peter Ensor is a precious and deeply-valued friend. He was amazingly crucial to each stage in the development of this book. In 2012 he was instrumental in my being invited to deliver lectures on Modern Church History at Cliff College, England (in association with the University of Manchester). Later, he connected Janet and me with Kenya

Methodist University, where we filled a teaching gap between 2015 and 2017. We lectured there for three Trimesters (one Trimester per year); so by August 2017 we had completed a full academic year of teaching! Our young theology students in the university (most of whom are preparing for ministry in the church in East Africa) have been a huge source of inspiration to us both. Kenya Methodist University was where this book really found its genesis.

There are so many others to whom we owe a debt of gratitude. Professor Alec Ryrie at Durham University has given generous help and warm encouragement over the last 4 years. He also kindly provided much-appreciated academic criticism of Chapters 3 and 4. Dr Olubunmi Olayisade is the Africa Secretary of the British Methodist Church: Janet and I have greatly valued her help and friendship. Over the last 10 years we have been part of the Cliff College International Training Centre Core Team, under the direction of the Revd Richard Jackson as its Coordinator. We have been inspired by his combination of visionary initiative and efficient administration, as we have travelled round Nigeria, as well as visiting Sierra Leone and Uganda, under the Cliff College umbrella.

It would indeed be spiritually churlish if we failed to acknowledge the huge debt we owe to the myriad of people who have prayed for us deeply and regularly; including for the publication of this book. In particular, we need to mention our own dear Minister and his wife in this Scottish glen: the Revd Jannie du Plessis and Sunet. They are South Africans, and have spent most of their extensive ministry in varied settings within and around their country of birth. No one could have better understood the setting of this book; and no one could have better or more prayerfully encouraged us. We thank God for them.

But most of all we want to honour the God and Father of our LORD Jesus Christ, and give Him all the glory for this book. With the Psalmist, we would exclaim:

"Not to us, O LORD, not to us, but to Your Name be the glory, because of Your love and faithfulness" (Psalm 115: 1, NIV).

The old Authorised Version translation of the last part of the verse also resonates deeply:

"unto Thy Name give glory, for Thy mercy, and for Thy truth's sake".

It has been said of John Wesley's organization of his Methodist societies that he received it 'piece-by-piece from heaven'. It would be dishonouring to our LORD God to say anything other about the production of this book. To His Name alone be all the praise and all the glory!

USE OF BIBLE TRANSLATIONS

New Revised Standard Version (anglicised edition), (OUP, Oxford, 2003) ISBN 0 – 19 – 100016 – 7 (In the book's text, quoted as **NRSV**)

King James Version (the usual description in the USA): **The Authorised Version** (the usual description in the UK). In this book, quotations are from The New Chain-Reference Bible (ed. Thompson, F.C., Kirkbride Bible Co, Indianapolis, 1934). (In the book's text, quoted as **AV**)

New International Version (anglicised edition), Thompson Chain Reference Edition, (Hodder and Stoughton, GB, 1984). (In the book's text, quoted as **NIV**)

New Living Translation (British Text), Living Water Edition) (Tyndale House Publishers Inc., Wheaton, Illinois, USA, 2000). (In the book's text, quoted as NLT)

INTRODUCTION

In the book title, the phrase 'from an African perspective' is an important element. "For what you see and hear depends a good deal on where you are standing: it also depends on what sort of person you are"[1]. A historian rejects these limitations at his peril. Perspective inevitably affects perception: when the context is altered, the content is affected. So it has been with these present studies. Loving Africa (as my wife and I do), the following chapters were originally prepared as lectures, over a three-year period, for delivery at the Methodist University of Kenya. This focussed preparation has affected in depth my understandings of what Modern Church History is about. I had not realised that my historical orientation was hitherto sub-consciously 'euro-centric'. To view modern church history from outside the European continent has altered my understandings considerably.

When gazing at mountain ranges geographically, 'where you are standing' inevitably affects how you see the topography in which you are placed. When it comes to surveying the historical landscape, the same principle applies. Viewing the European Reformations from the standpoint of sub-Saharan Africa has caused some landmarks, considered indisputably significant in a European context, to be diminished in importance. However, other features have taken on a higher profile. For example, the biographies of Luther invariably mention his happy marriage to 'my Katie'. But in a continent where 'marriage is the primary issue' [2], the amazing growth of Christian faith has brought marriage into new focus as a key concern. Therefore, in the African context, Luther's understandings of marriage cannot but become a particular focus of attention in a new way. This is not to say that Reformation history is to be reinterpreted in the light of contemporary Africa! As Professor Herbert Butterfield once noted, history is not to be written with 'one eye, so to speak, upon the present'. This author is simply affirming that new insights are gained when history-writing is undertaken from outside the confines of a single continent.

Another change of perspective impacting these studies has been the recent development of 'ethnographic history', concentrating on the viewpoint of ordinary people involved, and thereby creating new understandings of modern church history. Traditionally, history has been studied in terms of causation and consequence, and the narrative has been seen through the eyes of the 'key players'. Little attention has been given to the understandings and responses of ordinary people in the communities involved. But ethnographic history attaches priority to new questions like: What did the events mean to the mass of the participants? What was their 'world view'? What did <u>they</u> believe was going on? [3]

A whole set of subsidiary questions also emerge from this new perspective: How did participants understand the nature and extent of spiritual authority and civil government? How did they relate all this to Bible narratives and teachings? What 'direction of travel' were the ordinary participants undertaking: what (if any) were their goals, both spiritually and politically? How far were they willing to go? What difference did all this make to the participants' understanding of individual responsibilities and social duties? Indeed, how was their perception of society itself being challenged? Perhaps the deepest question is this: 'What driving forces led ordinary folk (as well as their leaders) to risk everything –sometimes even willingly sacrificing their lives – for the cause to which they were committed?'

There are several recurring questions underlying the succeeding chapters with their descriptions of reformers, revivalists and prophets over five centuries: How far were these leaders consciously introducing new understandings and practice? In their own thinking, were they simply 'correcting' imbalances, corruption and unbiblical thinking which had grown up in their regional churches? In their self-understanding, were they simply rediscovering the norms of Christian life and faith which they observed in the pages of the New Testament? To cite just one example, when John Wesley produced a pamphlet describing the character of a 'Methodist', he concluded that he was describing no other than the basic beliefs, practices and lifestyle of normal Christianity as represented in the pages of the New Testament. How far was this true of other church leaders over the centuries? And how far might this affect our historical assessments of them and the movements with which they are associated?

An understandable criticism of the chapters which follow is that they are too limited in analysis, naïve in judgements and over-specialized in scope. The writer would accept this criticism to a degree. However, the purpose of this explorative work is not to provide yet another full history of the subject. Rather, it is to observe some main features of that history from a different, African perspective, thereby highlighting several features of that history which have either been neglected, dismissed, or misunderstood in past historiography. In all this, the first aim has been to help African students, who often come to the subject with little background in European history or Western culture. If the result has been a selectivity and over-simplification which readers from other backgrounds might find almost offensive, so be it. They will have whole libraries of books to consult, which offer a more traditional narrative and analysis. This book is not written for them. However, just as the writer has found new features and new continuities to explore as a result of an 'African perspective', so also the hope is that other Western readers might catch his enthusiasm. Indeed, the writer's greater hope is that some of the conclusions tentatively expressed in this work might be further explored within contemporary mainline historiography.

It has been provocatively affirmed: 'The future of Christianity ... is African' [4]. The writer longs that this present book would be of some use in enabling African readers better to estimate the significance for themselves of the last five hundred years of global Church history. Perhaps, too, it will provide a fresh perspective for readers from Western cultures. My prayer is that for all who use it as a tool to explore the complex, invigorating narrative of Modern Church History, it will act as a signpost, pointing to a deeper awareness of the Truth.

NOTES AND REFERENCES

[1]   Lewis, C.S, <u>The Magician's Nephew</u>, (The Bodley Head, 1955) p.131

[2]   Quoting the opinion of an African-born leader in the British Methodist Church, who has crossed and re-crossed sub-Saharan Africa during recent years

[3]   In this shift of emphasis, the author wishes to pay tribute to the writings of Professor Alec Ryrie. His ground-breaking book, <u>Being Protestant in Reformation Britain</u> (OUP, Oxford, 2013) has been especially appreciated

[4]   Quoted in <u>The Economist</u>, January 2015

CHAPTER ONE

MARTIN LUTHER AND THE BEGINNINGS OF RADICAL CHANGE, 1517 – 1546

"By faith alone"

"Born Anew"

The year is 1505, over five hundred years ago. The place is within the modern state of Germany. Here is a young man suddenly engulfed in a life-threatening crisis. He finds himself in woodland when a sudden severe thunder-and-lightning storm overtakes him. He thinks he is going to die, and vows that he will enter into the monastic life if he is spared. The young man, Martin Luther, did not die, neither from being struck by lightning nor by a falling tree, and he kept his vow. He joined an Order devoted to St Augustine. (Some would say that, apart from the Scriptures themselves, Augustine has played a more formative role in the development of Western Christian thought than any other individual.) Necessarily, therefore, Luther would have met up with Augustine's central teaching: salvation is entirely by grace - all we can do is to believe, to have faith[1]. The year 1515 found Luther lecturing on Paul's Letter to the Roman Christians, and coming to see that faith was central to salvation: "For I am not ashamed of the gospel; it is the power of God for salvation to everyone who has faith … For in it the righteousness of God is revealed through faith for faith; as it is written, 'The one who is righteous will live by faith'" (Romans 1: 17 NRSV, quoting Habakkuk 2: 4).

1

In Luther's Latin Bible, the Vulgate translation, 'righteous' and 'righteousness' were translated 'justus' and 'justitia'; therefore justification is understood to mean being 'put right with God'. But for Luther, the agonizing question was how could such a miracle happen? How could a sinful human be put right with God? Little by little, Luther came to the conclusion that justification is through faith alone, and that the 'justice of God' does not refer, as he had been taught, to the punishing of sinners. It means rather that the righteousness of believers is not their own but God's. This righteousness of God is given to those who live by faith in the crucified and risen Jesus. It is given, not because they fulfil the demands of divine justice, but simply because God wishes to give it. Therefore, both faith and justification are free gifts from God to sinners. "I felt myself," said Luther, as this revelation gripped him, "to be reborn and to have gone through open doors into paradise. The whole of Scripture took on a new meaning".

Later, Luther translated the New Testament into his own native language of German. When he came to Jesus' discussion with Nicodemus, to translate Jesus' own words in John 3: 7, Luther used the German expression "Ihr musset von neuem geboren werden" (You must be born anew). This closely reflects his vocabulary in describing the change that occurred to him in his own inner being when he first understood this Gospel heart-truth. The Latin phrase Luther used to describe his own experience was "Hic me prorsus renatum esse sensi." An early translator of Luther's writings into German rendered "renatum" as "wiedergeboren" (born again) – a very similar German expression to that which Luther had used to translate John 3: 7. Luther's whole life was totally renewed and entirely changed by the revelatory truth that both justification and the faith to receive it are gifts from an overwhelmingly gracious God. And Luther saw what can only be called his 'conversion experience,' as identical with Jesus' own imperative to Nicodemus. So this sense of being 'born anew,' or 'born again', this rediscovery of the very core of the Good News of Jesus, was at the heart of the Protestant Reformation from its inception[2].

The Western Church, with Rome as its administrative centre, had developed the practice of selling indulgences. Indulgences were sold for money, with the popular understanding that, from the gifts of the faithful, remissions from pain in purgatory could be bought – either for oneself or for loved ones already deceased. "The moment the money tinkles in the collecting box, a soul flies out of purgatory": this proverb was actually preached to encourage the sale of Indulgences at that time! In 1517, Luther proposed a University disputation in Wittenburg on Ninety-five Theses, which he nailed to the door of the church building. In these theses, he strongly criticised the practice of selling indulgences. His great concern was that he could not square indulgences with God's gracious gift of faith. Later, around 1530 Luther began to speak out against the whole concept of purgatory. Clearly, faith could not be bought for money!

His opponents saw his actions as rebellion against authority, and they wanted to affirm Church discipline. In 1520, Luther was excommunicated. He burned the excommunication edict in Wittenburg, cheered on by students and townsfolk; clearly, by now he had a popular following. Far from being silenced, Luther took a hugely significant step: he started to proclaim and print his message not only in Latin but also in German, the language of the ordinary people. Luther took advantage of the recently-developed printing press to turn out large numbers of quickly-printed pamphlets. Thus, to use an idiom from the internet-age, Luther's message 'went viral!' In fact, Luther was the first person in history to make full use of printing as a means of widely publicising his views, and he was one of the first to write with the printed page in mind.

In 1519, Charles V had been elected Holy Roman Emperor. Still a teenager, he ruled the largest Empire the Christian West had ever seen, and he had a serious-minded concern to do what God wanted. He heeded Luther's protector, Friedrich of Saxony, and gave the increasingly well-known Luther an opportunity to present his views at the first available meeting of the Diet (the regular imperial assembly), at Worms in April 1521. Luther told the Emperor that he could not recant what he had said and written, without a conviction from "scripture or plain reason (for I believe neither in Pope nor councils alone)." Luther's editor later included two tiny summary sentences which are always associated with Luther: "Here I stand: I can do no other." In the months following the Diet, Friedrich arranged for Luther to be hidden away in a secure place, and during those months Luther began his translation of the Bible into German [3].

Luther and Bible Translation

Luther's translation of the New Testament was significant for four reasons. First, his translation was based on the original Greek, and so provided a more accurate translation than if it had been based on the Latin Vulgate translation. Translating from the original language directly into the vernacular was naturally the better method. Second, Luther was a master of the vernacular, sensitive to the rhythms of everyday German. His powerful, urgent use of language was both terse and emotional. His translation influenced the whole development of the German language. Always a man of the people himself, he deliberately aimed at making his translation accessible and clear to the ordinary person. By translating and publishing the New Testament into German, Luther opened up the Scriptures to anyone who was literate and had money enough to buy a copy for themselves. Now, potentially, everyone would have access to the Bible, not just priests and theologians. Third, Luther's New Testament was 'mass-produced' through the relatively recent development of the printing press. (Gutenberg first began using movable print around 1450; Caxton established the first printing press in England in 1476). Luther's New Testament was first published in September 1522, but it had to be reprinted within three months, so popular did it prove. (In December of the same year, Luther completed the whole Bible in German, and that was finally published in 1534.) One of Luther's opponents later complained that the common people loved it and old women studied it and argued about its texts: it was perhaps the greatest compliment that Luther could have been paid. The new printing presses were also used to publish Luther's books and tracts, so that news about his opinions could be quickly disseminated amongst the whole German-speaking world and beyond. The fourth significant point about Luther's translation of the Bible was his ultimate aim that ordinary folk should experience in their own lives the power of the evangelical Gospel, as he had rediscovered it in his own life. For this purpose, his Bible in German - the Scriptures in the language of the ordinary people - was fundamental. His desire for 'ordinary people' to have their lives transformed by the Gospel is evidenced in the way he translated Romans 3: 28. He added the word "alone" so that it read, "justified without works of the law, by faith **alone**" (my emphasis). In doing this, Luther believed that he was simply making clear the true intent of the verse, and <u>that</u> was the meaning he wanted to communicate to others Between 1534 and 1584, one hundred thousand German Bibles were produced by one Wittenberg printing press alone, each copy insisting that we are put right with God 'by faith alone'[4]. Luther's central message was actually embedded in the translation itself!

Luther's theology of 'the Word' was a critical element in the development of the Reformation. By the time of his appearing before the Diet of Worms in 1521, he had already come to his main theological conclusions. Crucially important was his attitude to the Scriptures. His understanding was that the Word of God went deeper than the actual written words in the Bible. Christ Himself is the very Word of God incarnate. "Jesus Himself is God's greatest revelation and God's greatest action." Therefore, for Luther, "it was neither the church that made the Bible, nor the Bible that made the church. Final authority rests neither in the church nor in the Bible, but in the gospel, in the message of Jesus Christ, who is the Word of God incarnate" [5].

Luther and Political Authority

As well as 'taking on' the Church hierarchy, Luther's understandings of 'justification by faith alone' led him to take issue with the humanism being expounded by such intellectually able scholars as Erasmus. Erasmus insisted that humanity retained free will to respond to God's offer of grace: when Adam and Eve fell in Eden, their God-given capacity to reason had not been fully corrupted, only damaged. Luther replied uncompromisingly in his tract <u>On the Slavery of the Will</u> (December 1525) to the effect that human beings could expect nothing but condemnation and had nothing whatsoever to offer God that could merit salvation. "If we believe that

Christ redeemed man by His blood," he wrote, "we are forced to confess that all of man was lost".

Often, this early phase of the Reformation is called the Magisterial Reformation. The political rulers of the small states which made up much of the Holy Roman Empire cooperated with Luther and his local associates to introduce sweeping religious changes into the areas over which they had political control. Inevitably, then, religion and politics became inextricably inter-connected. By 1525, large areas of Europe saw revolts by farmers and peasants. These were called Bauernkrieg (Peasants' War or Farmers' War) – revolts against princes and Church leaders. Luther was horrified, and applauded the rulers' brutal suppression of the disorder. Romans 13: 1 - 2 became a key text for him and for other reformers: "Let every person be subject to the governing authorities; for there is no authority except from God, and those authorities that exist have been instituted by God. Therefore whoever resists authority resists what God has appointed, and those who resist will incur judgement" (NRSV). The repercussions from this emphasis, it may be argued, were still being felt in Germany 400 years later [6].

Other huge political changes began to occur as a result of the growing ecclesiastical and theological turmoil. In 1525, Albrecht of Brandenberg-Ausbach encouraged his cousin, King Sigismund of Poland, to remodel his territories as a secular fief with Albrecht as the new Duke of Prussia. Albrecht had met Luther in Wittenburg in late 1523, and was sympathetic to his cause. As a result, in summer 1525, an evangelical state-church came into being, under the protection of a secular ruler. This was the first of its sort in Europe, but within a comparatively short time, there were to be more examples – with developments in England being particularly significant. In the succeeding decades, various local rulers of regions within the Holy Roman Empire became allied to the 'Protestant' cause, whilst others (including the Emperor Charles himself) retained their allegiance to the Rome-based Catholic Church.

The encouragement, protection and support of state-rulers became crucial to the new 'evangelical movement'. By the late 1520s, Charles V (the

Holy Roman Emperor) had turned against Luther and his programme, and these sentiments were expressed in statements made at the Imperial Diet in 1529. In 1530, a group of German princes and other supporters of Luther presented a very moderate statement of doctrine, protesting against the anti-Luther statements of the previous Diet. As a result, they were nicknamed 'Protestants'. Their statement of doctrine was not accepted by the Emperor – but the nickname stuck [7]. Over the next twenty or thirty years the Empire became irrevocably divided. So, in 1555 the Diet of Augsburg accepted a settlement in which the religious complexion of any given territory would be decided, not by the Emperor, but by the territorial ruler. The principle was 'cuius regio, eius religio': the ruler determines the religion.

Luther and Marriage

The strength of the new order, where rulers had a powerful voice in spiritual matters was demonstrated by the Landgrave Philip of Hesse, who had pursued relationships with a string of mistresses after being married at the age of nineteen. His conversion to Protestantism sadly failed to alter his life-style, and in 1539 he became attracted to a seventeen-year-old aristocratic girl. Her mother demanded that any marriage should only be by permission of Protestant leaders of the church. So Philip applied to Luther and his colleagues Melanchton and Bucer. Luther and Melanchton sanctioned Philip's second marriage on the grounds that the Patriarch Abraham had more than one wife. Not surprisingly, many godly folk were unimpressed by this argument, and Luther himself later said that if he had known about Philip's previous behaviour, he would never have sanctioned the marriage. Some Catholics, as well as some in the Protestant groups, shared Luther's view that bigamy was preferable to divorce. But the whole incident reflected unfavourably on some aspects of the Protestants' relationships between political power and spiritual authority. It heralded many more problems and challenges to come!

Luther's own marriage was much happier. As his 'pastoral theology' developed, he began consistently to teach that vows of lifelong celibacy were both unscriptural and unnatural, but never considered marriage was for himself personally. However, during the Peasants' War, when life was in turmoil for him, and there was a price on his head, he suddenly married an ex-nun, Catherine von Bora. He enjoyed a happy family life thereafter, with six children. "I love my Katie; yes, I love her more dearly than myself": in such words he clearly stated his love [8]. Many friends were welcomed into his home. He once said, "Next to God's Word there is no more precious treasure than holy matrimony." "Luther would say that his family was like a 'small church,' and would rejoice in being part of it … His efforts to educate his own children as well as others have been cited as a forerunner of public education. Furthermore, Luther's family life became the model that many devout Germans would follow for generations" [9].

Some have suggested that, following Luther's lead, from this time on, European cultures little-by-little embraced romantic love (eros) as an essential component of a happy marriage. It has been argued that "Luther inaugurated a cultural paradigm shift in the very concept of marriage … Luther's marriage reconfigured the reason for marriage from a consideration of dowry and social status to mutual affection" [10]. It may also be noted that the provision of an heir was often, from patriarchal times, a main consideration in marriage - the behaviour of King Henry V111 in England providing a distasteful example of treating wives as heir-providers, with little respect or love for them as human beings. It may be an exaggeration to suggest that, through Luther's very different understanding of marriage, European cultures began to embrace romantic love as an essential component for a happy marriage. Undoubtedly, however, Luther's abandonment of celibacy in favour of a fulfilling, loving marriage provided a powerful statement theologically and a striking example culturally in the early years of the Protestant Reformation.

Is there any substantial evidence that the example of Luther's own marriage did in fact forcefully affect the whole Protestant understanding of marriage? Inevitably, the evidence will be fragmentary and anecdotal. However, there is one clear indicator, at least in relation to English Protestantism. The early 16th. Century provided the first opportunity, for those who could, to invest in books and reading, because the growing number of printing presses meant books were being 'mass-produced' for the first time. Professor Alec Ryrie, in a scholarly and deeply-researched book, affirms that the first English Protestant book which could properly be termed a 'best-seller' bore the title: "The christen state of Matrimonye, wherein housbandes and wyfes maye lerne to kepe house together with love." It was translated into English from the German by Miles Coverdale in 1543. Its author was Heinrich Bullinger, who succeeded Zwingli as the leader of the 'city-state' of Zurich, and was one of the formational architects of Reformed theology and practice. Bullinger's influence was crucial in the development of the Reformed group of churches [11]. He himself must have been influenced by Luther's theological stand. Was he also influenced by Luther's understanding of marriage? Were Bullinger's last three words of his book on marriage – "together with love" – indicative of a new awareness that 'love' was an essential ingredient of a Christian marriage? Perhaps he was simply taking his cue from Scripture passages on sexual love within marriage which are to be found in such books as Proverbs and Song of Songs? These tantalising questions may never be answered. Yet, incontrovertibly, 'with love' – implicitly referring to 'eros love' as a God-given blessing – was impressed upon the perception of marriage from the Protestant movement's earliest days.

Luther and Work

In 1520, Luther wrote in revolutionary style about 'work' in his tract The Babylonian Captivity of the Church. "The works of monks and priests, however holy and arduous they be, do not differ one whit in the sight of God from the works of the rustic labourer in the field or the woman going about her household tasks, but that all works are measured before God by faith alone." "When a man changes a nappy, affirmed Luther, God and the angels smile!"[12].

Statements such as these by Luther have aroused much discussion about the relationship between the rise of Protestantism and developing understandings about ordinary work. Especially in the 20th Century, considerable research was undertaken concerning 'the Protestant work ethic'. Titles of widely-read books reflected this discussion, starting with Max Weber's The Protestant Ethic and the Spirit of Capitalism [13]. However, by the beginning of the 21st Century, it was widely accepted that Weber had, at the very least, overstated the relationship between the advent of Protestantism and the development of capitalism.

Perhaps the 20th Century academic debate about possible links between the rise of Protestantism and the growth of the 'market economy' has obscured a simpler, but more significant point about Luther's attitude to work. For him, ordinary work had an autonomous value and inherent dignity because it was God-ordained. This attitude is well summarised in his famous and apparently contrary aphorism: "If I knew Jesus was returning tomorrow, I would still plant a tree today." Ordinary work is important not simply because of any useful productive outcomes, but because it reflects the very nature of the Creator, and basic principles of His creation.

Luther and Future Developments

In focusing on Luther's understanding of the Bible, political authority and marriage, other elements of Luther's work must not be overlooked; for example, his incipient reforms in social caring. "Part of Luther's genius was that he conceived of reformation broadly, not only in terms of theology, but also in terms of society" [14]. In Luther's understanding, when city councils and principalities assumed authority for the practice of religion, they also, by default, assumed responsibility for the poor and needy – a responsibility which, up to that time, had been undertaken by a variety of organizations under the covering authority of the Church. Such organizations included monasteries and mendicant orders, local parishes and wealthy citizens. Now hospitals and schools, orphanages and other institutions for poor relief were ultimately placed under the overarching authority of the state government.

One sad issue that comes to the fore in Luther's later life is his anti-semitism. In the 1520s he had adopted a tolerant and even respectful attitude to God's Old Testament chosen people. However, in 1543 he wrote a tract, <u>On the Jews and their Lies</u>, in which he urged the burning of Jewish synagogues, schools, and even homes. Jewish religious writings should be destroyed, and Jewish rabbis should be prevented from teaching. One can only speculate on what caused Luther's violent change of attitude. Many analysts would suggest that some reverberations from his anti-semitism could be seen in the modern state of Germany some four hundred years after Luther's death in 1546.

Luther, then, was not only a 'man of the people' in his ability to connect with ordinary people. He also carried some flawed – even dangerous – prejudices and understandings which were common to the people of his time. He was not the perfect and untarnished reformer that some might want to make of him. Yet his life and work were crucial to that movement which became known as 'The Reformation'. Courageously, he held on to his 'new', evangelical, biblical revelations concerning the nature of faith, and they were fundamental to the triggering of the Protestant Reformation. It would not be an exaggeration to summarise his significance thus: 'No Luther, no Reformation'.

NOTES AND REFERENCES

"By faith alone" in the chapter sub-title is Luther's own rendering of Romans 3: 28. The original Greek does not contain the word "alone." (There is further discussion of this point in the main body of the text.)

[1]   MacCulloch, Diarmid, A History of Christianity (Allen Lane, London, 2009) ISBN 978 – 0 – 713 – 99869 – 6, ps. 606–7

[2]   "Luther at 500: An essay on Luther's Reformation": article in The Economist, 4 November 2017. The crucial point that Luther felt 'born again' or 'born anew' is routinely emphasized in biographical writing about Luther. See, for example, Gonzalez, Justo, The Story of Christianity Vol. 2: The Reformation to the Present Day (New York, Harper One, 2010) ISBN 978 – 06 – 185589; p. 25. However, for the present writer, The Economist article highlighted the essential 'new birth' dimension of Luther's personal spiritual journey in a way that no other description has managed to do.

The translator referred to in the text, who rendered Luther's Latin into the German, was Johann Georg Walch (1693 – 1773). Walch's translation from the Latin 'prorsus' he rendered 'ganz' (completely) in the German. It would seem no exaggeration, therefore, (if Walch rightly understood Luther's words in Latin) to take 'ganz wiedergeboren sei' as indicating that Luther found himself 'completely born again/anew'.

[3]   MacCulloch, op. cit., p. 611

[4]   Woodbridge and James, Church History Vol. 2: From Pre-Reformation to the Present Day, (Zondervan, Grand Rapids, Michigan, 2013) ISBN 978 – 0 – 310 – 25743 – 1 (v. 2), p. 129. They wrongly cite the verse as Romans 3: 38: it is in fact Romans 3: 28

[5]   Gonzalez, op. cit., p. 48. Luther's understanding of 'the Word of God' as the place where Jesus meets us helps explain why Luther could dismiss the Epistle of James as 'pure straw'. He was not ready to delete it from the canon of Scripture, but he found it of little value because he did not encounter Jesus in it.

[6]   Reference may be made to the anti-semitism of the Nazi Party in Germany in the 1930s and 1940s.

[7]   MacCulloch, op. cit., p. 621

[8]   Woodbridge and James, op. cit., p.141

[9]   Gonzalez, op. cit., p.43

[10] Woodbridge and James, op. cit., p.141

[11] Ryrie, Alec, Being Protestant in Reformation Britain (OUP, Oxford, 2013) ISBN: 978 – 0 – 19 – 956572 – 6, p.296. Perhaps Bullinger's greatest achievement

was the production of the Second Helvetic Confession of 1561. See Woodbridge and James, op. cit., ps. 157 – 158

[12] Guiness, O., <u>The Call</u> (W Publishing Group, Thomas Nelson, Nashville, Tennessee, 1998) ps. 33 – 34

[13] This whole debate is briefly and helpfully summarised in MacCulloch, op. cit., p. 1108. The summary is located in the last paragraph of his notes on 'non-magisterial' impacts of the Reformation in Northern Europe.

[14] Woodbridge and James, op. cit., p.142

AFRICAN PERSPECTIVES: SOME DISCUSSION POINTS

1   "The Reformation began not with Luther's act of defiance, with a poster on Wittenberg's Church door, but with a 'new birth' in his own heart." In other words, radical outward action by Luther was preceded by transformational inward change. How does this relate to you own personal experience?

2   Luther's translation of the Bible into German, his native language, is generally recognised to have been one of his most significant achievements. Why was it so important to have the Bible translated into the vernacular, and then made widely available, in 16th and 17th. Century Europe? How would we estimate the importance of Bible-translation in sub-Saharan Africa, especially during the 19th and 20th Centuries?

3   Discuss Luther's use of Romans 13: 1 - 7, and its outworking over succeeding centuries. What are the benefits – and what are the dangers – of Luther's approach? How may it relate to present-day political realities in Africa?

4   It has been said that Luther's own marriage radically recalibrated the whole Protestant understanding of marriage. A prominent African Christian leader recently said, 'The biggest issue in Africa is marriage.' How may Luther's recalibration impact our contemporary understanding of marriage in Africa?

CHAPTER TWO

SYSTEMATIC THEOLOGY, POLITICALLY APPLIED: THE DEVELOPING REFORMATION, 1525 – 1564

"For by grace you have been saved"

Introduction

Calvin represented a different generation from Luther; born only twenty-six years after Luther's birth. Calvin continued to exert a growing influence in the development of the Protestant Reformation until his death in 1564, almost twenty years after Luther's own death. Before turning our full attention to Calvin, however, some background is needed about the Holy Roman Empire in the first half of the 16th Century in western and central Europe. Many of the cities in the Holy Roman Empire were like free city-states, and the new Reformation teaching soon influenced some of them. The results were to be seen in cities such as Strasbourg, Nuremberg, Bern and Zurich. Typically, the leading citizens were attracted to the new teaching, and legislated to reform the local churches and parishes. When the bishop tried to interfere, they repudiated his authority. Soon, some city councils were becoming more radical and revolutionary than Luther would have comfortably allowed, Zurich providing a good example of that.

Ulrich Zwingli (1484 – 1531) in Zurich

Zwingli was born in Switzerland, and in 1506 (at the age of twenty-two) he became a village priest. By the time he was transferred to Zurich, he had reached a theological position similar to that of Luther. However, his 'route to such conclusions had not been the anguished quest of the German Reformer, but rather the study of Scripture . . . . Later, Zwingli would declare that, even before having heard of Luther's teachings, he had come to similar conclusions through his study of the Bible. Thus, Zwingli's reformation was not a direct result of Luther's; rather it was a parallel movement' [1.] The Zurich city council (on the advice of Zwingli and the chief pastors in the city) legislated to allow clerical marriage; to remove superstitious images and relics; to suppress the monasteries and use their endowments for education; to order a simplified liturgy in the vernacular instead of the Mass in Latin; to control public morals with reforming regulations.

Because this reformation was in collaboration with the city magistrates, local reformations like that in Zurich were often entitled 'Magisterial Reformations'. There were three particular areas within which the city states quickly became more radical in their reforming zeal than Luther's original 'evangelical movement' would have supported. First, there was a new understanding of authority, especially in relation to the Bible as the Word of God. Luther's attitude inclined to the view that nothing in worship and practice should be contrary to the Word of God. Zwingli's attitude was to do only what was explicitly sanctioned by the Bible; in this distinctive way he emphasized the primacy of Scripture. (This significant difference between Luther and Zwingli represented a "fault-line" which continued to have huge consequences through the subsequent centuries of Protestant church history.) Zwingli also began preaching in a distinctive way. Instead of preaching from appointed lectionary texts, he expounded the Bible verse by verse, chapter by chapter – an expository method sometimes called lectio continua. Not surprisingly, therefore, Zwingli's way of proceeding tended to greater simplicity and plain-ness. Even hymns and songs were thought to be unscriptural, and only metrical versions of the Psalms were sung (as in the Free Church of Scotland in later centuries). A second radical departure from the past concerned a new attitude to images, which had not been a focus of Luther's concern. In Zwingli's Zurich, religious pictures and sculptures and relics were all sold, removed or destroyed, together with organs and ornate altars. (A comparison with the attitude of Puritans in 17th. Century Britain, and Islamist extremists in the 21st. Century, may not be out of place.) Third, The Mass, Eucharist, or the LORD's Supper became in Zurich a simple symbolic meal, served from a table placed in the middle of the nave, by ministers wearing ordinary lay clothes. The host was not elevated to present the bread as an offering before God. Zwingli concluded that Jesus' words, "This is My Body" meant, "This is a sign of My Body" – in the same way that "I am the Vine" or "I am the Door" were to be understood [2].

In 1531, Zurich ill-advisedly went to war with the Swiss Catholic Cantons, and Zwingli, sword in hand, was killed in battle at Kappel. In Zurich, his place was taken by Heinrich Bullinger, who proved to be an outstanding leader. Bullinger's crowning achievement was the Second Helvetic Confession (1561). This document became the most influential and widely accepted confession of faith among those churches which later became known as 'Reformed churches'. [3] It was accepted in the Palatinate, France, Hungary, Poland and Scotland. Meanwhile, Zwinglli's theology and practice were being further developed in another Swiss city, Geneva.

John Calvin (1509 – 1564) in Geneva

Calvin arrived in Geneva in the late 1530s, having fled from persecution in Paris, and began to confront the Geneva City Council with a programme of desirable reforms. One 'consuming passion of his life was hatred of public mess,'[4] and the Council soon proved unwilling to implement his ideas, expelling him from the city in 1538. However, he was recalled in 1541, and from then on, his life focused on the reform of the church and city-state of Geneva. In his first sermon on returning to Geneva, he emphasized his determination to establish the Geneva church "as is prescribed in the Word of God and was in use in the early Church". The Geneva church – and, therefore the city state of Geneva – were to be established on the firm foundation of Scripture. The great 'method' which Calvin employed in pursuing this reformation of Geneva was preaching. For Calvin, the pulpit was a sacred place, and he spoke of a 'hidden energy' that takes the words of the preacher beyond his preparation to reach the hearts of the listeners. 'For Calvin, preaching had a kind of sacramental quality in which the Holy Spirit – the hidden energy - is actively present and communicating grace to the people' [5].

Church Elders – disciplinary officials – were the most distinctive of Calvin's institutions. They were appointed by the Council of the City Government after consultation with the pastors. Every Thursday the Elders were to meet with the pastors in Consistory and consider any disorder in the church which required a remedy. In other contexts, the consistories were called presbyteries, which is why churches organised along the lines pioneered by Calvin in Geneva were often called 'presbyterian'. They were there to admonish the sinner; and if the sinner was still impenitent, they might excommunicate him and inform the magistrate.

There was little 'democracy' in Calvin's ideal (or, as he would have understood it, his scripturally-based) church. But there was an uneasy relationship between the city council (the 'temporal' authority) and the institutions of the church (the 'spiritual' authority). These boundaries, always difficult to define, became a hugely significant issue in countries like England and Scotland in the 16th and 17th Centuries. But in Calvin's Geneva, the city government largely backed the spiritual authority of the Church; and the Church largely proscribed the moral behaviour of the population. 'Calvinism' – which began (like so many religious labels) as an insult – began to denote, in social terms, a severe and inflexible code of communal regulation and regimentation. John Knox, who spent time in the city called Calvin's Geneva "the most perfect school of Christ that ever was on earth since the days of the Apostles."

In 1553, a prominent radical intellectual arrived in Geneva: Michael Servetus. He was from Spain and, like Calvin himself, an exile. Servetus denied that the doctrine of the Trinity could be found in Scripture. He had already been condemned as a heretic by a Catholic inquisition. Calvin saw it as his duty to put Servetus to death. 'Thus Calvin established that Protestants were as determined as Catholics to represent the mainstream traditional Christianity which had culminated in the Council of Chalcedon'6. (Chalcedon was considered by many of the new Protestants as the last general council of the church to make reliable scripture-based decisions.)

Calvin's wider influence in Western Christendom was extended because of his Institution of the Christian Religion – usually referred to as the Institutes. This was a textbook which combined a clear theological system with thorough biblical exposition. Until then, most Protestant literature had dealt exclusively with the particular points at issue: Calvin's Institutes provided a systematic framework of Protestant theology. It was first published as a short manual in 1536, but Calvin steadily extended it through numerous editions; the final edition, before his death in 1564, was published in 1559. By then, the Institutes had grown to a work of four books containing eighty chapters!

Luther's great Bible verse was "The just shall live by faith" (Romans 1: 17, AV): Calvin's, "By grace" (Ephesians 2: 8, NRSV). For Calvin, God's special grace providentially guided all the events of the world – even the apparently insignificant events: "Are not two sparrows sold for a penny. Yet not one of them falls to the ground unperceived by your Father" (Matthew 10: 29, NRSV). There is no place for luck or chance. Everything – literally everything – is ordered by God's will. Therefore, another key verse for Calvin was, "Thy will be done" (Matthew 6: 10, AV). Much of this would be agreed by Luther and by any Protestant – indeed, by any Christian. Christian thinkers, especially those of the Pauline and Augustinian tradition, had been taught that they could not deserve heaven, nor achieve it by effort: rather, the Christian life was to be accepted through faith as a gift of God's mercy and love. Moreover, God chose some and not others. For them, Scripture taught it and observation confirmed it. This tradition also maintained that everything is a gift of God; our part is simply to have faith to receive it – though even faith is in itself a gift of God.

However, Calvin saw God's grace with a new focus –and came to a new severe understanding of how God's grace operates among humankind. In Calvin's theology and practice, God's sovereign grace provided a crucial element which gave the whole of life a new perspective. God's grace became the keystone of his theology: all was seen through this prism. Calvin pursued the doctrines of Sovereign Grace, God's Providence and Predestination through to their logical conclusion – though perhaps also drawing extended conclusions which are not made fully explicit in Scripture, and therefore not wholly backed by biblical authority (see, for example, Romans 11: 32). 'In proclaiming this majestic doctrine Calvin stripped from it the whispering hesitations of his predecessors. He could write nothing obscurely – and therefore he wrote plainly the awful consequences' [7]. Chadwick has summarised these 'Calvinist' consequences: "that Christ died on the cross not for all mankind, but only for the elect; that God does not will all men to be saved; that men were created by God whom he decreed from all eternity to be consigned to an eternal destruction' [8]. The positive 'flip-side' of all this was that the Elect could not lose their salvation; and this powerful doctrine of election became ever more important to the growing number of 'Reformed' Christians in succeeding centuries, comforting and empowering them.

Partly because of the severity of those sections of the <u>Institutes</u> dealing with predestination, and partly because of the harshness of the judgement meted out to Servetus, Calvin has been traditionally understood as a person without much human compassion or emotional sensitivity. You might admire him or hate him, but you could hardly love him. However, in his personal life and in his pastoral ministry in Geneva, Calvin did display tender affection. His wife died young, and left him deeply grieving this tragic loss. Yet, in the same year as his wife died, he mentioned in a letter how he had daily visited a dying woman in his congregation. He adds his own pastoral reflection: 'We ought to weep with those who weep. That is to say, if we are Christians, we ought to have such compassion and sorrow for our neighbours that we should willingly take part in their tears, and thus comfort them' [9].

Perhaps, too, Calvin's attitude to what Protestants in later centuries would call 'world mission,' has been misunderstood. It has been assumed that the strength of any evangelistic and missionary vision would have been curtailed by the harshness of Calvin's doctrine of predestination. In fact, Calvin confronts this objection head on in the <u>Institutes</u> (111.23.24) by quoting the words of Augustine: "For as we do not know who belongs to the number of them predestined or who does not belong, we ought to be so minded as to wish that all men be saved." Calvin then adds: "So shall it come about that we try to make everyone we meet a sharer of our peace." In the last decade of Calvin's life, more than 2,150 Protestant churches were planted in France with the help of the Church in Geneva; and by 1564, at the time of Calvin's death, it has been estimated that there were around three million Protestants in France. An attempt was even made to establish a Protestant colony in what is now Brazil. In 1557, two Geneva-sponsored missionaries landed in the present-day Rio de Janeiro. Although this project came to nothing, the very fact that it was attempted suggests the strength of a 'world mission' concern in Calvin's Geneva [10].

By the end of the 16th Century, the Protestantism of the likes of Zwingli and Calvin would be called 'Reformed'. This term was largely used to cover all varieties of non-Lutheran Protestantism. This 'Reformed Christianity' began to spread through many European ethnic groups, but Lutheranism remained largely confined to the Germanic and Scandinavian cultures. At the same time as this development of Reformed churches was taking place, the Catholic Church – now generally known by Protestants as 'the Roman Catholic Church' – was also experiencing reformation. This movement is usually termed the Counter Reformation, but may be better described as the Catholic Reformation. This reformation process was largely facilitated by the Council of Trent. This Council first met in 1545, and lasted for almost 20 years, concluding in 1563. It resulted in a reaffirmation of the Pope's authority over the church. But it also enabled the flourishing of reforming missionary orders such as the Jesuits. This great movement deserves a separate book.

Anabapists in Switzerland, Germany and Holland

The two questions which any radical, revolutionary cause must eventually ask are, 'What is our goal?' and 'To what extremes are we prepared to go, in order to achieve our goal?' As the reformation developed, two influences began to affect ordinary people. First, more people became literate. Second, the Bible became readily – and comparatively cheaply – available in the vernacular, the common tongue of the people, made possible partly through the invention of printing. So, many an ordinary 'Protestant' man began to see the Bible in the light of truth imparted by the Spirit – that same Holy Spirit who had brought him to faith in Christ. He discovered that there were many other issues illuminated by Scripture, in addition to the doctrine of 'by grace through faith'. Many little groups came into being with a wide variety of doctrines and practices. They tended to be 'lumped together' as 'Anabaptists' (that is,'re-baptisers') because some of their most articulate leaders denounced infant baptism [11].

In 1525, the first known Anabaptist 'adult baptism' of the Reformation era took place in Zurich. Early in 1527, Felix Manz, who had conducted the baptism, was condemned to death by drowning by Zurich city officials. Why such severe treatment from fellow Protestant believers? It may help to recall Zwingli's dictum, 'A Christian city is nothing other than a Christian church'. No distinction was made between the state and the church; indeed, infant baptism was understood as not only a religious rite of entrance into the church, but also as a civic rite of entrance into citizenship of the Swiss canton. Therefore, advocating the need for adult baptism was seen as a serious dividing of the community into opposing factions [12].

In 1527, the Anabaptist Confession of Schleitheim was drawn up – the nearest thing to an agreed document amongst these diverse groups. It proclaimed adult baptism, and declared that the sacrament of communion should be offered only to those who, having repented and amended their lives, had been baptised as adults. It insisted on separation from all that is not united with God in Christ, which meant in practice separation from 'the world.' It renounced enforced attendance at parish churches. It condemned the use of force – 'the sword' – or going to law: indeed, becoming a magistrate or taking oaths was forbidden. Not surprisingly, the outside world – especially political authorities – viewed the AnabaptIsts with horror.

As all the first Reformation leaders reacted strongly against the Anabaptists, it is worth considering in a little more detail the reasons for their antipathy, which, at first appearance, might seem strange. After all, the New Testament contains no explicit example of infant baptism; and if baptism was a sacrament of repentance and faith in Christ, it was self-evident that infants could not personally fulfil these conditions. Yet, as has been recounted, Reformers like Zwingli in Zurich turned violently against the Anabaptists. Zwingli, like both Luther and the Papacy itself, held that all society should be part of the Church in Christendom. Therefore, to opt for baptism as an adult was to split the wholeness of the community, into believers and non-believers. For Zwingli, the Church of Zurich embraced the whole city of Zurich. Likewise, for Calvin, the Church of Geneva evidently encompassed the whole city of Geneva. From the purely political aspect, these Reformation leaders liaised with kings, princes, city councils and magistrates in bringing about change in a state or a city. The Anabaptists were in effect challenging this whole edifice, and their beliefs seemed to signal social disruption and political treason.

This violent opposition of the Reformed Church leaders towards the Anabaptists was reinforced by happenings in Munster in Westphalia in 1534 and 1535. A former Lutheran minister, Bernard Rothmann, gained control of the city council: he had become a radical Anabapist. Laws were passed to establish the sharing of goods, and polygamy was permitted, Rothmann himself taking 9 wives. An ex-innkeeper, John of Leyden, was proclaimed King of New Zion; wearing royal robes, he held his court in the market place. Most worryingly to the authorities in Europe, Rothmann issued a public incitement to world rebellion: "Dear brethren, arm yourselves for the battle … and annihilate the ungodly" [13]. This Anabaptist rebellion was brutally put down in mid-1535, but for decades to come, the name 'Munster' was in itself enough to delegitimize the doctrines and practices of even mild, tolerant and law-abiding Anabaptists. There <u>were</u> some such law-abiding Anabaptist groups who continued to believe in complete pacifism: the Mennonites, for example. They developed Christian communities in which the sharing of goods and resources was practised. Their descendants remained in Europe until the 19th Century, when they emigrated to the USA, where they still live in distinctive Christian communities.

NOTES AND REFERENCES :

"For by grace you have been saved" (Ephesians 2: 8, NRSV) in the chapter sub-title indicates the popular understanding of Calvin's distinctive theological stance concerning the nature of the Gospel.

[1]   Gonzalez, op. cit., ps. 59 – 60
[2]   Chadwick, op. cit., p.76
[3]   Reformed Churches have sometimes been designated Calvinist Churches
[4]   Chadwick, op. cit., p.92
[5]   Woodbridge and James, op. cit., p.167
[6]   MacCulloch, op. cit., p.633
[7]   Chadwick, op. cit., p.91
[8]   But see such texts as Ezek. 33. 11; 1Tim. 2. 4; and 2 Peter 3. 9
[9]   Woodbridge and James, op. cit., p.167
[10]   Ibid, ps. 175 - 178
[11]   Some Anabaptists in the Sixteenth and Seventeenth Centuries came to believe that no church was pure enough to baptise them, and so resorted to self-baptism. John Milton, literary genius and Cromwell's Secretary of State in Protectorate England, apparently came to believe that every individual was his own church.
[12]   Woodbridge and James, op. cit., ps. 154 - 155
[13]   Chadwick, op. cit., p.189. Also Gonzalez, op. cit., ps. 69 - 71

AFRICAN PERSPECTIVES: SOME DISCUSSION POINTS:

1   Luther tended to the view that a Christian – and the Christian community - should do nothing that was contrary to the Word of God. Zwingli's attitude was to do nothing other than what Scripture explicitly sanctioned. Would you incline to Luther's approach or to Zwingli's?

2   'A Christian city is nothing other than a Christian Church'. What do you make of Zwingli's dictum? What impact would such a principle have, if applied in contemporary Africa?

3   Calvin wrote that "Christ died on the cross not for all mankind, but only for the elect." Where do we stand? "Till all the ransomed church of God is saved to sin no more" (John Newton) <u>OR</u> "For all, for all, my Saviour died" (Charles Wesley)

4   A more general matter for consideration in the African context concerns the development of Anabaptists in the 16th and 17th Centuries in Europe. What happens when you have to stand up against the general flow and presuppositions of the prevailing culture in which you live? What happens when the Church seems apathetic, apostate, dead and unwilling to change – but yet seeks to impose uniformity on everybody?

CHAPTER THREE

A VERNACULAR BIBLE IN A 'MIDDLE-WAY' CHURCH, WITH DISCOMFITED DISSENTERS: THE BRITISH REFORMATION, 1534 – 1660

"Render . . . unto Caesar the things which are Caesar's; and unto God the things that are God's"

The Reformation in England

In mainland Europe, at least initially, the Reformation was focused on Christian faith: "by grace, … through faith" (Ephesians 2: 8, NRSV). In England, it was politically motivated by King Henry VIII (1509 - 1547). He was desperate to have a legitimate male heir to the throne and it seemed that his first wife, Catherine of Aragon, was never going to provide him with one. So Henry desired the Pope should annul the marriage. When the Pope virtually refused to do so, Henry began to look at the growth of Reformation doctrines as a means of satisfying his interests. Henry was a ruthless, tyrannical king, so it was not surprising that events in England seemed more cataclysmic in some ways than developments in continental Europe. For example, between 1536 and 1540, Henry closed and destroyed many monasteries, disbanding the Religious Orders. The reforms of Henry's reign resulted in a national church which was neither Lutheran nor Calvinist, but had a unique character: later, during the 17th Century, 'Anglican' became the accepted descriptor. Perhaps the concept became all the more distinct because England was part of an island: there could be little room for mistaking the original boundaries of 'Anglicanism'. Ultimately this distinctive expression of Reformation faith had a disproportionate impact on global Christianity in succeeding centuries, partly through the effect of British worldwide trade and Empire; partly because of the increasing use of the English language as a global 'lingua franca'. This impact continued over the succeeding centuries and, indeed, has become steadily more significant.

When the Pope, through endless prevarication, effectively refused to annul Henry's marriage to Catherine of Aragon, the king found a means of counteracting the authority of the Pope in his realm. From 1529 onwards, Henry widened further and further the meaning of the Statute of Praemunire (1352). In origin, this statute had been intended to exclude from the realm the effect of papal decrees when they interfered with the rights of English bishops. But between 1529 and 1531, it was absurdly extended to include all manner of other matters. Things moved so far so quickly that in 1531, the Convocations of York and Canterbury recognised the king as 'especial Protector, only and supreme Lord, and, as far as the law of Christ allows, even supreme Head[1]. By 1534, the Act of Supremacy declared the king was Supreme Head of the Church of England, and omitted the previous saving clause, 'as far as the law of Christ allows.' At this time, Thomas Cromwell had become the chief minister of state, and there was a new Archbishop of Canterbury, Thomas Cranmer, who was appointed in 1533. In mid-1535, Bishop Fisher of Rochester and Sir Thomas Moore, the ex-Chancellor, were both beheaded for refusing to swear to the royal supremacy in the Church, which diminished the Pope's authority in England. In 1540, Thomas Cromwell was executed because of his involvement with the king's further marriage plans, which did not work out to the king's satisfaction. But all through Henry's reign, Cranmer survived as Archbishop. This was partly due to his avoidance of intrigue or scandal; partly through his genuine belief in the doctrine of the godly prince; and partly because he was generally well-liked by all. Until Thomas Cromwell's execution, Cranmer and he worked together in a 'piecemeal dismantling of the old Church'[2].

Perhaps the greatest legacy to the English-speaking church out of these tumultuous decades was the dissemination, nationally, of a vernacular Bible. This Bible was produced by William Tyndale, an Oxford scholar, who made the English Bible his life's work. Tyndale was exiled to Antwerp, and King Henry's agents secured his kidnap: Tyndale was strangled and burnt at the stake near Brussels. But, only two years after Tyndale's death in 1536, surprisingly, it was Thomas Cromwell (rather than Cranmer) who secured a royal order for every parish in England to buy a complete English-language Bible, most of whose text was in fact Tyndale's translation (Henry V111 never seems to have realised this). "It is the ancestor of all Bibles in the English language, especially the 'Authorised' or 'King James' version'" [3]. 90% of the Authorised New Testament is Tyndale's!

The old king Henry died in 1547, and was succeeded by his nine-year-old son, Edward V1 (1547 – 1553). Protector Somerset, the real power in the land, was a friend of Cranmer and a supporter of reform. Various Acts of Parliament were passed, making it easier for the Protestant Reformers to spread their understandings of the Gospel. In 1547, injunctions were issued requiring the Gospels and Epistles to be read in English in church. In 1549, a new Prayer Book in the vernacular English was issued: this was altered over the next 3 years to produce the 1552 Prayer Book. Though these were the work of a Committee, Archbishop Cranmer's hand was firmly recognised in both. Neither of the Prayer Books satisfied everyone. The conservatives in the Church thought them too radical, the reformers thought them too conservative. But the 1552 Prayer Book moved closer to the vocabulary of the Reformers than the 1549 Book. Edward V1 died as a teenager, and was succeeded by Queen Mary (1553 – 1558). Mary's desire was to bring England back to the Catholic faith. Between the beginning of 1555 and her death in 1558, many reformers were burnt at the stake, including Archbishop Cranmer and four other bishops. The courage of the martyrs surprised the authorities and excited the respect and admiration of ordinary people. The steadfastness of the victims meant the English Protestant Reformation was now baptised in blood, and, as so often, the blood of the martyrs became the seed of the (reformed) church. In 1563, John Foxe, an English refugee living in Basle, published an English edition of his <u>Book of Martyrs</u>, celebrating those who had died for the Protestant cause. It was not always accurate, but was widely read in the succeeding decades – and indeed, the succeeding centuries – and had a strong 'anti-Rome' emphasis.

It has been suggested that in English minds in 1553, 'the Protestant cause was identified with church robbery, destruction, irreverence, religious anarchy,' but by 1558, it was 'beginning to be identified with virtue, honesty, and loyal English resistance to a half-foreign government.'[4] Mary's longed-for baby never came, so when she died in that same year of 1558, she was succeeded by her half-sister Elizabeth.

Queen Elizabeth (1558 – 1603)

The new queen's real religious beliefs were difficult to discern, but her advisers held to a moderate 'via media' or 'middle way', with a state church that was broad enough to accommodate most Protestants. For example, when a new edition of the <u>Book of Common Prayer</u> was issued, it combined two formulae which had been used separately in different earlier editions of the English Prayer Book: "The body of our Lord Jesus Christ which was given for thee, preserve thy body and soul unto everlasting life. Take and eat this in remembrance that Christ died for thee and feed on Him in thy heart by faith with thanksgiving"[5].

In 1571, Thirty-Nine Articles were promulgated, and assent demanded from the clergy. The Articles taught the classical doctrines of the Reformed Protestants: that men are justified by faith alone; that the grace of the sacraments is received only by men of faith; that nothing outside of Scripture is necessary for salvation. Over the years of Elizabeth's reign, moderation became the stance of the Church of England, worked out by such men as Richard Hooker. With a quiet reasonableness, he argued for the union of State and Church, with the right and duty of a godly prince to legislate in church matters as well as matters of state – always provided that his laws were in harmony with natural law and not contradicted by Scripture[6].

As Elizabeth's reign progressed and the 'middle way' in church affairs gained general assent, there developed a diverse group of serious-minded Reformers who lived a strictly moral life, fearing God and obeying the Word of God. Few were 'Lutheran' in mind-set, and many adhered to 'Calvinist' understandings of the Bible's teaching. They were sneeringly nicknamed 'Puritans'; but the name stuck and came into general use. These 'Puritans' were – at very least – uncomfortable with the late Sixteenth Century settlement of the Church in England. Before long, some began looking westwards, dreaming of new beginnings in a new world across the Atlantic Ocean. Among these Puritans who began to think about leaving England and its 'religious compromises' were small radical 'extremist' groups who rejected altogether the apparatus of the state church. For most of these small congregations, the concept of <u>covenant</u> became fundamental (as it was also to become for a substantial body of Christian believers in Scotland). Each member bound themselves to a solemn covenant with God, which involved commitment to a holy lifestyle, and on the basis of this covenant, a moral discipline was exercised by all members of the congregation [7].

As news of a new world on the other side of the Atlantic grew, some intrepid sailors and traders began to think of pioneering permanent settlements on the new continent's eastern littoral. Some harassed Puritans had been distressed by their exclusion from the state church, as a result of limits imposed by the Elizabethan settlement. Their eyes began to turn westwards with hope in their hearts of better things. In 1620, (nearly two decades after the end Elizabeth's reign), the ship <u>Mayflower</u> sailed for Massachusetts. There were other settlements established around this time not only in the bleak conditions of Masssachusetts, but also in Conneticut, New Hampshire, and Rhode Island. Maryland was given a charter in 1632, and attracted Roman Catholic refugees. For the Protestant settlers, their crucial understanding for the way forward was that the Scriptures should be pivotal in their new polities. The Bible would act not only as the basis for doctrine and church government, but also for the whole of life. They were not just looking for a new start: they were literally looking for a New World, and in that new world, the Word of God would be central. John Robinson, preaching to the church before the <u>Mayflower</u> voyage, said he was very sure that "the Lord had more truth and light to break forth out of His holy Word".[8]

The Reformation in 16th Century Scotland: 'The People of the Covenant'

(Note: Scottish Church Reformation history is dealt with in greater detail in the following chapter) [9].

From 1542, Scotland's monarch, was Mary Queen of Scots – not to be confused with the other Queen Mary who ruled England from 1553 to 1558. Because Mary Queen of Scots was a woman, and also a minor, the lordly landowners of the Kingdom wielded great power. In 1557, a group of lords, calling themselves the 'Lords of the Congregation', formed themselves into a 'covenant', a group committed to defending the Word of God. In 1560, Queen Elizabeth of England sent money, ships and an army to Leith in support of this Reforming party. Thereafter, the Scottish Parliament repudiated the authority of the Pope, abolished the Mass in Scotland, and accepted a Calvinist Confession of faith drafted by John Knox. Knox had spent time in Calvin's Geneva, where he was much impressed by the organization of that City State. He returned to Scotland with his famous appeal to God in prayer, 'Give me Scotland or I perish!'

Mary Queen of Scots was a Catholic, and it became ever clearer that she could not rule an increasingly Protestant (Calvinist) nation. 'Cuius regio eius religio', means 'the religion of the ruler is the religion of the nation'. In the 16th and 17th Centuries this became an axiom. But it became increasingly obvious that a weak ruler could not govern a nation against the strongly-held faith of the people. In 1567, Mary was forced to abdicate and was succeeded by her infant son, James V1 of Scotland.

James VI of Scotland; James I of England (1603 – 1625)

When Queen Elizabeth died in 1603, she was succeeded by the Scottish King James V1 of Scotland, who now also became James I of England. All his life, James had struggled with the claims of the Scottish presbyteries against the crown's authority. On his accession to the English throne, he famously affirmed the principle, "No bishops, no king." This policy – already firmly established in England – he also attempted to implement in Scotland.

James' most memorable achievement in relation to Protestant Reformation was to set up a group of some 47 scholars to produce an improved rendering of the Scriptures into English. They were instructed to follow the 'Bishops' Bible' of 1568: in fact, they adopted some of the work of other translations. The result was the 'Authorised' or 'King James Version' of the Bible, produced in 1611 – surely the most enduring and influential book ever printed in the English language. It was authorised in the sense that it was 'appointed to be read in churches', as its title page states. Other versions were not made illegal, and indeed the 'Authorised Version' only won full acceptance slowly. But over the remainder of the Seventeenth Century, little by little it was taken to be the 'standard' English Bible translation, with its depth of scholarship and amazing literary power.

In his relations with both the English and the Scottish Parliaments and Churches, James acted slowly and wisely. However, in 1625, James was succeeded by his son Charles I (1625 – 1649), who was neither cautious nor wise. As Charles attempted to impose more and more episcopalian symbols in Scotland, more Scots resisted the changes, and with increasing determination. In 1638, many Scottish folk signed the <u>Scottish National Covenant</u>, swearing to uphold their presbyterian understandings of Church organization. These signatories became known as 'Covenanters'. Two successive 'Bishops' Wars' broke out against the monarch as a result. In 1643, the Scots bound themselves in a <u>Solemn League and Covenant</u> with the English Parliamentarians. They agreed to get rid of 'prelacy' and to introduce a presbyterian form of church government in both England and Scotland.

Civil War, Oliver Cromwell, and Independents in the Army, 1642 – 1660

In England, the Civil War broke out in 1642, and (after a peaceful year in 1647) finished by the end of 1648. From 1643, the English Parliament allied with Scotland, and that military alliance (as has just been described) drove the Commons to accept more of the Presbyterian system into the church in England. In fact, it looked as though England might fully accept church government of a Presbyterian complexion. But as the New Model Army became the chief political force in the country, it was 'Independency' that became the ecclesiastical watchword. Oliver Cromwell himself (by then the key national political and military leader), together with many of his colonels, were Independents. They believed in liberty of worship for all, with no enforcement of the regulations of a state church, nor of a national presbyterian system, let alone of a Pope in the Roman Vatican. Among their soldiers, officers in Cromwell's Army often conducted prayers and preached sermons. Indeed, Cromwell hoped that each regiment would become a 'gathered church'. Some opinion in the Army became very radical indeed. A small section of the soldiers, calling themselves the 'true Levellers', demanded sweeping social change: "Unless we that are poor have some part of the land to live upon freely as well as the gentry, it cannot be a free Commonwealth." Prominent among these radical groups were the Fifth Monarchists. They focused their attention on Daniel Chapter 2: 44, and intended to be agents to bring in the promised monarchy 'from God in heaven'. The worry among more moderate people was that they would try to use force to do so!

In 1647, debates were held in St Mary's Church, Putney between the soldiers and officers of Oliver Cromwell's 'New Model Army', chaired by Cromwell himself. The most senior officer to side with the radicals, Colonel Thomas Rainsborough, famously voiced ideas of universal suffrage which may be considered 'centuries ahead of their time'. He said: "For really I think that the poorest hee that is in England hath a life to live, as the greatest hee; and therefore … every Man that is to live under a Government ought first by his own Consent to put himself under that Government." Authority was to be vested in the House of Commons rather than the King and Lords. Certain 'native rights' were declared sacrosanct for all Englishmen: freedom of conscience, freedom from conscription into the armed forces and equality before the law. These debates might be understood as the consummation of the English Reformation in its impact upon the political and social affairs of the nation [10].

In those mid-years of the 17th Century, some earnest English readers of Scripture began to move towards increasingly radical spiritual concepts. They began to insist that **all** external religious forms were unnecessary, and even harmful. Set patterns of liturgy were rejected by some Independents, in order that worship might be totally free. Some groups of 'Seekers' simply waited communally for the direct inspiration of the Spirit, and rejected even the Sacraments and the reading of Scripture. The only one of these groups which survived much beyond the 17th Century was 'The Society of Friends', also known as the 'Quakers' – led during the Protectorate by George Fox.

The end of the English Civil War left a major European state under a military leader who favoured Independency. The result was a degree of religious toleration and freedom which had not been known before, and was not to be repeated by the civil authority for several centuries. Although Cromwell favoured godly puritanism, his government allowed a huge variety of religious ideas and understandings. He even (in an attitude generally foreign to the 17th Century) wanted toleration for the Jews, allowing them to meet in private houses for devotion, and showing them encouragement and favour. One of the most notable Independents in the administration was the Secretary of State, John Milton – also one of England's greatest literary geniuses. He helped to provide an intellectual foundation in favour of Independency. However, with the return of King Charles II in the Restoration of 1660, episcopacy was restored and the 'Church of England' was again recognised as the 'state church'. But the years of Oliver Cromwell's Commonwealth and Protectorate meant that from then on, 'the Dissenters' (who would not accept control by a state church) had to be recognised as a permanent element in the land.

NOTES AND REFERENCES:

"Render therefore unto Caesar the things which are Caesar's; and unto God the things that are God's" (Matthew 22. 21, AV) perhaps most succinctly represents (in the words of Jesus Himself) the tension inherent in the developing Reformation in England.

1   Chadwick, op. cit., p.100
2   MacCulloch, op. cit., p.626
3   Ibid., p.627
4   Chadwick, op. cit., p.11
5   This point is well made by Gonzalez, op. cit. p.97
6   Woodbridge and James, op. cit., ps. 237 – 242
7   Ibid., ps. 242 – 244
8   Ibid., p. 271
9   Fuller Notes and References for the Scottish Reformation are provided in the following chapter, Chapter 4
10   Ashley, M., The Greatness of Oliver Cromwell (Collier Books, New York, 1962), ps. 192 - 195

AFRICAN PERSPECTIVES; SOME DISCUSSION POINTS:

1   "Render to Caesar what is Caesar's, and to God what is God's." How have these words of Jesus been 'played out' in sub-Saharan Africa over the last 200 years in the relationship between Christian faith and the wielding of political power?

2   The word 'Independent' was first used – as a term to describe models of church organisation – in Cromwell's Commonwealth, especially in his New Model Army. The exponential rise of 'African Independent Churches' in the early 21st Century has been one of the distinctive features of the numerical growth of Christianity in that continent. Are there any elements of comparison with the 'Independency' of Cromwell's England? Or are 'AICs' a totally new and distinctively African development?

3   By 1660 in England, 'Dissenters' had to be recognised as a permanent, distinctive element in the church and in society. How should modern African states deal with religious "dissent"? Are there limits to how much dissent should be allowed? If so, how should dissent be limited?

CHAPTER FOUR

A COVENANTED NATION
THE REFORMED CHURCH IN
SCOTLAND, 1546 – 1688

**"Pursue love, and strive for spiritual gifts, and
especially that you may prophesy"**

A Brief Outline: Scotland, America and Africa

In the 16th and 17th Centuries, Scotland was a small state on the northern
edge of the European Reformation. Its citizens were divided into querulous
and opposing factions and clans (tribes). Yet its Reformation history is
globally significant for three reasons: First, it became the only national
'Reformed Church' which accepted that the prophetic and miraculous
dimensions of faith recorded in the New Testament were still relevant
and available to Church congregations and to individual followers of
Christ in the succeeding centuries. The prophetic became common in
the life and ministry of many early leaders in the Scottish Reformed
Church. Signs and wonders, healings and miracles were frequently
recorded in primary sources. Prophecy was particularly prominent as a
gift valued by the Reformers. Second, as early as the mid-seventeenth
century this Scottish experience was crossing continents, first of all to the
'New World', where its influence may still be discerned in the 'American
Evangelicalism' of later centuries. The third reason for Scotland's global
significance – and most significant for Africa – this process of crossing
continents continued through the succeeding three hundred years. In the

Nineteenth Century, there was a succession of Scottish missionaries and explorers whose influence was widely felt across sub-Saharan Africa. Their own Scottish heritage is therefore of considerable interest in the context of 'global Christian mission'.

George Wishart (1513? – 1546)

Wishart was the 'father' of the Scots' tradition of prophetic utterance. Much of what we know of Wishart comes through the pen of John Knox, Wishart's better-known successor. It is significant in itself that Knox, as an acknowledged shaper of Scotland's Reformation, had such a tremendous respect for Wishart that he wrote a hagiographical biography. Knox describes (in old Scottish spelling) how Wishart was *so clearly illummated with the spreat of prophesye, that he saw nott only thingis perteanyng to him self, but also such thingis as some Tounes and the hole Realme afterward felt.* Professor Alec Ryrie has summarised the evidence on which Knox's statement was based: "The plague which hit Dundee did so four days after Wishart had cursed the town for silencing his preaching there. When he drew a meagre audience in Haddington, Wishart pronounced judgement of fire and sword against the town, which within five years was flattened." More encouragingly, albeit less specifically, he prophesied to his friends that a full and perfect reformation would come to Scotland. Clearest of all, he foresaw his own death. When an assassin had tried to murder him, Wishart foresaw it and was able to intercept and disarm the man: for it was not yet his time. 'When that time came, he repeatedly preached that he was about to die; and when they came for him, he was ready'[1].

John Knox (1513? – 1572)

At the time of Wishart's martyrdom, the Protestant cause in Scotland was by no means secured. Though there were communities of Protestants in Ayr and Dundee, 'the Protestant cause in Scotland was carried on mainly through loosely knit conventicles'[2]. However, in 1559, John

Malcolm McCall

Knox returned permanently to his native Scotland having spent time in Calvin's Geneva. His vision for Scotland was clear, uncompromising and passionate: "Give me Scotland or I die," was his fervent prayer. Political circumstances provided Knox with his opportunity. By 1560, as head of a committee of six theologians, he had issued a 'party manifesto' in the form of a <u>Confession of Faith</u>. Much of this Confession was soon implemented. A General Assembly was called together, and it confirmed a service book after the Geneva model, known as <u>The Book of Common Order</u>. In 1554, this book was printed with the metrical psalms included. Organizationally, a system of 'presbyteries' was introduced into local parishes. Kirk Sessions, composed of the minister and elders of the local congregation, were instituted to oversee the spiritual, social and moral discipline of the community. 'Reformed ministers' were installed in many parishes. The worship of the church was transformed. The greatest focus in pursuing reform in worship concerned the theology and ritual of the Mass. The Reformers 'dedicated themselves to re-creating Christ's Last Supper as they envisioned the Evangelists and Paul having received it [3].

Knox thus achieved a considerable transformation in Scottish Church life in accordance with the principles he had seen operating in Calvin's Geneva. In one respect, however, Knox set the Scottish Kirk on a course utterly distinctive from all the other Reformed Churches in mainland Europe. In line with his huge admiration and respect for Wishart, John Knox accepted that the 'prophetic word,' described in the New Testament, was an ongoing gift of the Spirit of God in contemporary Church life and ministry. Indeed, in later life, John Knox affirmed himself to be a prophet. Along with prophecy, the Scottish Reformers also recognised the reality of "signs and wonders and various miracles, and by gifts of the Holy Spirit" (Hebrews 2: 4, NRSV). Thus Knox's work followed seamlessly the ministry of George Wishart, in which all these elements were present. In the Scottish Presbyterian Church there was thus established an 'apostolic succession' of preachers - men who were soaked in the prophetic tradition established by Wishart and Knox. They were led initially by John Welsh and Robert Bruce. John Welsh was Knox's son-in-law; Robert Bruce took up Knox's old post as minister in Edinburgh. Both these men were explicitly 'prophetic' in their ministries. For example, John Welsh was said to have been used to raise a dead person to life. On another occasion, faced with a 'popish' heckler, he called on the witnesses present to 'Observe the work of the Lord upon that profane wretch, which they should presently behold: Upon which immediately the profane wretch sunk down and died beneath the table' [4]. The result of these developments "was a tradition which set the Scottish Reformation apart from its neighbours: a most un-Calvinist tradition of prophetic utterance … *tradition* in the fullest sense of the word, a torch passed from generation to generation" [5]. In fact, it was more than a tradition of prophetic utterance only, because it involved healings and miracles, signs and wonders, as a wealth of primary sources reveal.

'Holy Fairs'

One significant element in this Scottish tradition became the large, open-air festive celebrations of the Lord's Supper. From the 1590s onwards they became an essential annual part of the Presbyterian calendar in some areas of Scotland – notably in the South-West and the 'Central Belt'. These celebrations took place mainly in Summer or early Autumn – necessarily at this time of the year, because of prevailing weather conditions in Scotland! One of the most famous of these 'Holy Fairs' took place at Shotts in 1630 under the leadership of John Livingston, a young Presbyterian preacher. A series of meetings continued "almost day and night, for four or five days." On the Monday, outdoors, the meetings culminated in an extraordinary "down-pouring of the SPIRIT." Livingston preached a two-and-a-half hour sermon, and it was said afterwards that many Christian leaders in that area "could date either their *conversion*, or some remarkable *confirmation* in their case from *that day*." It was also recorded that many were so overwhelmed at this time that they fainted away and laid on the ground "as if they had been dead" [6]. It is worth mentioning that Robert Bruce – by that time an old man – was present at this gathering in Shotts: his ministry spanned the years 1587 to 1631, providing a visible thread of continuity between the era of John Knox, and the spiritual renewals and revivals of 17th Century Scotland [7].

Professor Eric Schmidt has convincingly demonstrated that these celebrations were not only a domestic Scottish phenomenon. They were taken to Ulster (the northern part of Ireland) by 'refugee' or 'planter' Scottish Presbyterians and their ministers. Thereafter, they were carried by Scottish Presbyterian ministers to the American colonies. Here they provided a long-term element in the development of the 'Camp Meeting' which was a characteristic feature of early American evangelicalism. This transcontinental transmission of 'Holy Fairs' provides the reason for the sub-title of Professor Schmidt's book, <u>Scotland and the Making of American Revivalism</u> [8].

A Covenanted Nation

Back in Scotland, the English king, Charles I (1625 – 1649), tried during the 1630s to bring the Scottish Church in line with the Anglican tradition which had already developed in England. His father, James I, had acted slowly and wisely: Charles was neither cautious nor wise. Charles attempted to impose an episcopal organization on the Scottish church, and to introduce a new Prayer Book for use in Scotland. Such 'innovations' ignited Scottish opposition. In 1638, the Presbyterians drew up a National Covenant, which was signed by huge numbers of ordinary Scots, as well as their ecclesiastical and political leaders. The Covenant bound the signatories to resist all ecclesiastical innovations which might be understood to lower the unique position of Jesus as sole King over His Church. In practice, this meant opposing the episcopal system which gave King Charles a privileged place in the Church as the 'Supreme Governor'. Those signing this document became known as Covenanters. Fiercely Scottish and Presbyterian, the Covenanters were suspicious of all things English and Anglican. A present-day historian, Neil Oliver, has emphasized the significance of the National Covenant: "For the first time in history the ordinary men and women – the mass of us – were briefly visible"[9].

Despite serious disagreements among themselves and with their English Puritan counterparts, the Covenanters remained a substantial force in Scotland throughout the 1640s. In 1643, the English Parliamentarians and the Scottish Presbyterians bound themselves together to extirpate prelacy and to introduce a Presbyterian form of Church polity in England and Scotland. In 1651 Charles II, at his Scottish coronation, reluctantly promised Scottish leaders that he would sign and swear to the Covenant, and much was hoped from a 'Covenanting king'. However, after his Restoration in 1660 the new king was not true to his word, and quickly moved against the Covenanters. Episcopacy was rapidly re-established. Around three hundred Presbyterian ministers were turned out of their parishes. Some of these ministers started leading 'conventicles': open air meetings and communions in secluded places within the hills of South-West Scotland, not unlike the 'Holy Fairs' of a previous generation. These gatherings, however, were declared illegal, but yet they were attended by hundreds – even thousands – of covenanting Scots. In opposition to this movement, covenants were burned and ministers ordered either to resign or be banished. These non-conformists were fined, tortured, flogged, branded or even executed without trial. South-west Scotland was the heartland of resistance, as mercenary armies, led by ambitious Scots who were subservient to the English monarch, traversed the region.

One of the covenanting leaders was Alexander Peden (1626? – 1686). In the 1660s he became one of the men most wanted by the government. He is a prime example of the continuing Scottish presbyterian tradition in ministry which was accompanied by prophecy, with miraculous signs and wonders. Some events in Peden's ministry are recorded by John Howie, in his <u>Biographica Scoticana</u> (1775). For instance, Peden was imprisoned on the Bass Rock, near Edinburgh, in 1673 with sixty other Covenanters. In 1678, they were sentenced to be transported to the American colonies, never to see Scotland again. Yet Sandy Peden averred that the ship was not yet built which should take him and these prisoners to Virginia, or any other of the English plantations in America. They were put on board a ship to take them, initially, to London. The ship's skipper was about to pass them over to another sea captain who was to take them to Virginia. However, when this second captain "found they were all grave, sober Christians, banished for Presbyterian principles, he would sail the sea with none such. In this confusion, as the one skipper would not receive them, and the other would keep them no longer at his own expense, they were set at liberty" [10]. Howie recounts another incident when the sick Peden was being sought by the authorities. The person hiding him in his house felt that it was too dangerous for Peden to stay indoors, so he made him a bed in a nearby field, hidden among the grain which was almost ready to be harvested. In the night, there was a great deluge of rain, with flooding. Yet not a drop of rain was seen within ten feet of the outdoor bed where Peden had lain! [11]

These 'killing times' intensified under the rule of King James II (1685 – 1688), who was James VII of Scotland. Many Covenanter leaders were arrested, exiled or killed. An estimated 18,000 died in 25 years. Of those who lived, many were sold as slaves to America or entombed in dungeons. Often these martyrs were young men, little more than teenagers. Other Covenanters – especially some covenanting Ministers - fled to Holland and England. Then, with the accession of William of Orange in 1688, the period of terror was suddenly over: but many a graveyard tombstone tersely and fiercely records the deaths of those covenanters during the 'killing times:' for example:

> "Here lyes James Bennoch, shot by Col. Duglas
> and Livingston's Dragoons at Englston
> for adhering to the Word of God,
> Christ's kingly goverment in His Church,
> and the covenanted work of Reformation
> against tyranny, perjury and prelacy.
> April 28 1685.
> Rev 12. 11" [12].

Possibly the last martyr on British soil was young James Renwick of Moniaive. At the age of twenty, he was secretly sent to Holland to study for the ministry. Between 1685 and 1688 he exercised a powerful though unlawful ministry in the open air throughout the moors and glens of South-West Scotland. He was hanged at Edinburgh in February 1688 at the age of twenty-six. A few months later, King James abdicated the British throne, fleeing abroad from London in what became known as the 'Glorious Revolution'. In Scotland, the consequence was a speedy church settlement in which Presbyterianism was finally and firmly established as the accepted form of church in Protestant Scotland.

Historical Apodosis

It has been said that there have only been two peoples in history who, as whole nations, have covenanted themselves to God: Old Testament Israel and modern Scotland. Recently, at a church history conference in Scotland, one Presbyterian minister, referring to the present-day, remarked, 'The Covenant must mean <u>something</u>'. The contention of this study of the Scottish Reformed Church is that it did indeed mean 'something' – consciously or subconsciously - for succeeding generations of Presbyterian Scots. For example, it can hardly have failed, at some level, deeply to have influenced the lives of pioneers who missioned in 19th Century Africa. Scotsfolk like Mary Slessor and David Livingstone were inter-continentally recognised as Christian leaders, but they represented many lesser-known names too. These missionaries went into (for them) impossible situations in terms of climate, language, environment and alien culture. Many went knowingly risking their lives for the sake of the Gospel. Yet as single individuals, against all the odds, they made a lasting impression on the subsequent course of African church history. It might be said that their efforts were simply in line with a myriad of stories in the biblical narrative – from David and Goliath to Paul 'wrestling with wild beasts at Ephesus'. However, might not their lives and ministries also be seen to reflect a long-term thread in the particular tradition of the Reformed Church in Scotland? This thread clearly depended on the power of the Holy Spirit, and understood the 'gifts of the Spirit' to be available to contemporary Christians. This tradition – distinct from that of other European 'Reformed Churches' - was established in the lives of men like George Wishart, and continued in such covenanting heroes as Sandy Peden. It would indeed be surprising if elements of that same thread could not be discerned in the succeeding centuries of Scottish Church History.

CODA: LIVING AS PROTESTANTS AND 'DYING WELL' IN THE 16TH AND 17TH CENTURIES

"The assurance of things hoped for"

'Ordinary Protestants'

The first four chapters of these studies have covered aspects of the early Reformation period – roughly the century-and-a-half after 1517. They have largely concentrated on the lives of various significant individuals, relating their work to wider political, social and cultural changes. Some mention has already been made of the impact of these changes on ordinary people's lives. For example, Luther's understandings of marriage and of the value of daily work, when taken seriously, would necessarily have had an effect on people's everyday lives, as would his attitude to political authority and to the social responsibilities of civic authorities. Moreover, large numbers of ordinary people were unavoidably involved in Reformation-related conflicts and battles within their own regions, as their homelands turned into war-zones at various times during the early Reformation period. This was tragically true of those conflicts in mainland Europe which became known as the Thirty Years War (1618 – 1648). Again, for Protestants such as the Huguenots in France, or the Covenanters in South-West Scotland, suffering persecution for their faith, life was changed for ever. Obviously, life was also revolutionised for the handful of Protestants, like the English Puritans, who emigrated across the Atlantic to America.

Generally, however, in these first chapters, little attempt was made to engage with the daily lives of those ordinary people who now calling themselves 'Protestant'. This issue needs addressing now before moving on to studies of more recent centuries in subsequent chapters. The issue may be encapsulated in this question: What differences did their Protestantism make to individuals and to communities, both in their everyday living and in their perception of spiritual life-goals? And nothing can be more fundamental in this examination than recording changes to an individual's, or a community's, attitude to death – life's biggest mystery, greatest crisis, and final challenge. In fact, attitudes to death may act as a paradigm for more general developments in mind-set and behaviour amongst ordinary Protestants.

In a sense, all of earthly life is set against the backdrop of death and its significance. As many have observed, 'The only universal truth about human life is that one day we shall die.' Cultures have always recognised the ultimate significance of death, and made provision for its approach, though modern Western culture often tries to 'manage' death by pretending to ignore it! How did ordinary Protestant Christians in the first century of the Reformation view death as they moved through human life towards it? This reflection, seeking to uncover any changing attitude to death among 'ordinary Protestants', is largely drawn from Professor Alec Ryrie's book, Being Protestant in Reformation Britain. Naturally, therefore, the sources are English or Scottish-based. Of course, our knowledge will always be partial, because we have limited written sources to draw upon. It will also be fragmentary, because it depends on the records of those who were literate; and it can only highlight the personal understandings of those literate people who actually chose actually to write on this subject.

Throughout the early Reformation period, Christians of all persuasions – Protestant, Catholic or Orthodox - would have agreed that life was essentially a preparation for death. 'The wicked never think of death; but the godly think of nothing else': this might be taken as the typical comment of any serious Christian. A preacher's anecdote about a mortally-wounded soldier describes how the soldier was told not to fear death. "I thank God," he replied, "I fear not death, and these thirty years together, I never arose at the morning, that ever I made account [assumed] to live till night".

'Assurance'

The deathbed was 'the ultimate place of crisis and self-definition'. 'The point of death – when there is no longer any point in trying to fool anyone, but God must be confronted directly – was seen as one of the truest tests of sincerity'[13]. "Many ancient professors" died in spiritual confusion, (as one source records) because "they more respected men than God; and therefore in the time of death, when they must needs deal with God indeed, they know not what to do"[14]. Sometimes, a prophetic revelation about their imminent death was given to believers, providing an opportunity for them to put their house in order. Presumably, others were sometimes given an assurance concerning their return to health, that 'the sickness would not be unto death'.

The greatest, most natural, concern of the Protestant Christian in relation to death was the fate of the soul, not the body. The focus of the crisis was generally seen in the context of the final battle with the enemy, Satan. His temptations might include doubting the reality of one's faith. Judith Isham was "tempted with blasphemous thoughts . . . doubtings . . . and want of reverent believing". Becon, a profuse Protestant writer on the subject of death, noted how "Satan at the hour of death . . . would pluck thee from thine assurance and steadfast faith in Christ's blood and persuade thee that thou art but a damned wretch." In life, serious Protestants were most anxious to avoid hypocrisy and self-delusion in spiritual matters at all costs; so it would be surprising indeed if they were not confronted at death by attacks against their spiritual honesty and integrity. The "darkest valley" was the temptation to despair. The only way forward was to travel through this valley in the shelter of the merciful Shepherd's "rod and staff", until He brought the pilgrim into His everlasting heavenly banqueting hall.

Professor Ryrie summarises his careful research on how Reformation British Protestants viewed the subject of death and dying: "Many early Christians sought baptism on their deathbeds; their medieval successors looked to the sacramental trio of extreme unction, penance, and death-bed communion. The viaticum which early modern Protestants sought was assurance, and the sacrament which delivered it was a full-dress battle with, and final victory over, despair"[15]. Here indeed was a radical change of emphasis which Reformation thinking introduced into the considerations of one's personal death. Spiritual assurance was now the defence against fear and worry and was the greatly desired gift which strengthened the Protestant believer's resolve to 'die well.' So, in perhaps the deepest tectonic change of attitudes which the Reformation caused, the ministrations of the priest were replaced by a longing for 'full assurance of salvation' in the lives of countless numbers of serious Protestant believers. The initial battle-word of Luther's vocabulary, and the key-word for the subsequent Reformation was 'faith'. In the life-experience of Protestant believers, faith was amplified to encompass "full assurance of faith"[16]. Though in the pages of the New Testament, true faith is, in any case and by definition, "the assurance of things hoped for" [17].

Pilgrim's Progress

In line with all this, one final, strongly positive note on the subject of death and dying is provided by the writer John Bunyan (1628 – 1688). His writings summarise some of the central themes in the lives of zealous British Protestants in the early modern era. He memorably portrays the Christian life as a pilgrimage which contained one adversity after another, involving many temptations to despair, and, especially, constant battles with Satan and his minions. One of his characters faces death with these words: "'I am going to my Father's; and though with great difficulty I am got hither, yet now I do not repent of all the trouble I have been at to arrive where I am . . . . I have fought His battles who will now be my rewarder'. . . . So he passed over, and all the trumpets sounded for him on the other side" [18].

As Protestant believers during the early Reformation earnestly pondered the Scriptures on this subject, many must have been reassured by the writer to the Jewish Christians. He summarised the powerful effect of the supreme sacrifice of Jesus: "that through death He might destroy the one who has the power of death, that is, the devil, and free those who all their lives were held in slavery by the fear of death".[19] The Apostle Paul offers similar assurance: "Death has been swallowed up in victory!"[20]

NOTES AND REFERENCES:

"Pursue love and strive for the spiritual gifts, and especially that you may prophesy" (I Corinthians 14. 1, NRSV) in the chapter sub-title points to a distinctive feature of the Scottish Reformation.

1   Ryrie, Alec, "George Wishart: Scotland's Turbulent Prophet" in George Wishart Quincentennial Conference Proceedings p. 10 (ed. Martin Dotterweich, www. wishart.org, 2014) ISBN 978 -1 – 326 – 03932 – 5

2   Schmidt, Leigh Eric, Holy Fairs: Scotland and the making of American revivalism, (1989; second edition, with a new and valuable preface 2001, Eerdmans, Grand Rapids, Michigan) ISBN 0 – 8028 – 4966 – 0

3   Ibid., p.15

4   Ryrie, op. cit., p. 12. Schmidt, op. cit. p.22ff, also details such evidence from the lives of John Welsh and Robert Bruce

5   Ibid., p. 11

6   Schmidt, op. cit., p.21

7   Ibid., ps. 22 – 24

8   Ibid., see especially ps. 50ff

9   Oliver, N., A History of Scotland (Phoenix, Orion Books Ltd., by arrangement with the BBC, London, 2009) ISBN 978 – 0 – 7538 – 2663 – 8, p. 258

10 Howie, John, Scots Worthies, (first published 1775, revised by Rev W H Carslaw, Johnstone, Hunter and Co, Edinburgh, 1870) ps. 507 – 521

11 Ibid.

12 Transcribed from a Covenanter's gravestone in Glencairn Churchyard, Moniaive, Dumfries, Scotland. The name 'Duglas' and the word 'goverment' are clearly misspelt, suggesting that the rough-hewn gravestone was made by a local, unlearned mason from within the Glen. This might suggest a further detail of circumstantial evidence that the covenanting cause was indeed a 'people movement' espoused by ordinary folk. (Other gravestones from the same period spell 'government' correctly.)

    "The assurance of things hoped for" (Hebrews 11: 1, NRSV) quoted as the sub-heading of the Section on Living as Protestants and 'dying well' underlines how a key issue for early Protestants was the need for 'assurance'.

13 Ryrie, Being Protestant in Reformation Britain, ps. 462 - 468

14 Ibid., p. 462

15 Ibid., p. 468

16 Hebrews 10: 22 (NRSV)

17 Ibid., 11: 1

[18]   This quotation is from John Bunyan's <u>Pilgrim's Progress, Part 2: Christiana</u> (OUP, London, Oxford Standard Authors series, reprinted 1952) p. 368. <u>Pilgrim's Progress</u> became a hugely popular Protestant 'best-seller' in the English-speaking world. For more than three centuries it occupied a special place on the bookshelves of many earnest British Protestants, together with Foxe's <u>Book of Martyrs</u> and a copy of the Authorised Version of the Bible.

[19]   Hebrews 2: 14 – 15 (NRSV)

[20]   I Corinthians 15: 54 (NIV)

AFRICAN PERSPECTIVES: SOME DISCUSSION POINTS

1   Using the information provided in this chapter, reconsider the nature of the 'Holy Fairs' in Scotland which took place from the end of the 16th Century onwards. How might their spiritual significance be evaluated within the wider context of global Modern Church History? Do they suggest any parallels with African Christian experience?

<u>Note</u>: The present writer and his wife had the privilege in 2009 of sharing into the numerically largest African Methodist gathering ever held on the continent – in the open-air at Sagamu Methodist Training Institute, Nigeria. The parallels between this event and Schmidt's description of Scottish – and early American – 'Holy Fairs' were strikingly numerous.

2   The Scottish Covenanters were the last Christian martyrs to die on British soil. Which of the many African Christian martyrs have most inspired you?

3   Focus on the chapter's coda, entitled <u>Living as Protestants and 'dying well'</u>. Traditionally in Africa, beliefs and practice, and ceremonies relating to death have been accorded great importance. Estimate how the arrival of Christian faith in your local area affected and changed understandings of death and dying – and therefore the present ceremonies surrounding this subject. Are there any further changes which you would add to these understandings and ceremonies if you had the opportunity?

CHAPTER FIVE

"GOD HAS POURED HIS LOVE INTO OUR HEARTS BY THE HOLY SPIRIT": 18TH CENTURY MORAVIANS AND METHODISTS

Pietism and the Moravian Church

Early in the 15th Century, a hundred years before Luther's Ninety-Five Theses, a priest named John Huss became Rector of Prague University. He was greatly inspired by the prophetic and reforming message of the English Oxford scholar John Wyclif. In 1415, Huss was betrayed and burnt at the stake. Yet the movement he had started was never completely suppressed. The more radical followers of Huss ('Hussites') became known as the Union of Bohemian Brethren (Unitas Fratrum). In 1547, after further upheavals in Bohemia, the group took refuge in the Province of Moravia, and became known as the Moravian Brethren. In 1722, a handful of the Moravian Brethren were gathered together by a rich young nobleman, Count Nikolaus Ludwig von Zinzendorf, on his estate in southernmost Saxony (geographically far away from Moravia). He himself was only 22 years old at the time. A godly young man, he once observed: "I have one passion: it is Jesus, Jesus only".

In Saxony, a community village called Herrnhut (meaning 'on the LORD's watch', or 'under the LORD's watch') was developed as a place of refuge for the Moravians, a centre for worship and for farming and craftwork. However, by 1727 the community had sadly divided into warring factions.

Then, on 13th August 1727, the most amazing events happened during a communion service. At one point, Count Zinzendorf began publicly to confess the sins of the entire community, calling for rededication, and the gathered congregation began earnestly repenting of their sins. Zinzendorf described it as 'a day of the outpourings of the Holy Spirit … ; it was its Pentecost'. They experienced a pentecostal visitation of the Holy Spirit, accompanied by prophecies and visions, speaking in tongues and healings. The community was a group of mainly young people – Zinzendorf was now 27, about the average age of those present. They underwent a dramatic and almost indescribable transformation: Zinzendorf expressed it as 'a sense of nearness to Christ'. Others described it as the way in which they 'learned to love one another'. This has often been called the Herrnhut community's 'baptism in the Holy Spirit' or 'the Moravian Pentecost' [1].

Just two weeks later, on 27th August 1727, twenty-four men and twenty-four women covenanted to begin praying around the clock. They agreed that one man and one woman in separate places would pray in twenty-four one-hour shifts that would cover each hour of the day, every day of the week, and every week of the year. They all carefully observed the hour which had been appointed to them and they had a weekly meeting where prayer needs were expressed. Mostly they prayed for revival and the spread of Christian mission to every corner of the world. Soon, this little Moravian community was ablaze with a passion for world mission: in 1732 its first missionaries left for the Caribbean. It has been claimed that 'within a period of twenty years a movement that had begun with two hundred refugees had more missionaries overseas than had been sent out by all Protestant churches since the Protestant Reformation two centuries earlier' [2]. Little by little thereafter, over the next two centuries, a network of Moravian communities spread out across Russia, Britain, and into the New World. All this mission dynamic was sustained by the non-stop '24/7' Prayer Meeting - which lasted for a hundred years! [3]

It may be also helpful to relate the Moravians into the wider context of the 'Pietist' movement. The Moravians were, in fact, among the most notable groups of Christians who, in the late 17th and early 18th Centuries, became known collectively as 'Pietists'. They were characterized by, <u>first,</u>

an emphasis on personal holiness. They focused on a religion of the heart through a personal relationship with Jesus. In some ways these informal groups reflected the old monastic tradition, often **covenanting** themselves together in large extended families. Second, Bible-reading, prayer and (especially) hymn-singing were at the heart of the daily life of these groups. The basic message they proclaimed was of Jesus' redemption of sinners through His shed blood on the Cross. In his emphasis on the Bible, Zinzendorf (and, later, John Wesley) was influenced by Jakob Bohme's thinking. Bohme emphasized the need to encounter 'the living Word, through which the heart experiences certainty'[4]. Third, they generally withdrew from the political structures and economic organization of the societies in which they lived, pursuing their own simple, separated, distinctive lifestyle. Finally, education was considered very important to them – or perhaps, more specifically, they deeply respected an intellectual ability and training which could cogently expound the Scriptures, read theology, and apply all this to 'the signs of the times'.

Nevertherless, the missionaries they sent out were often humble and uneducated lay folk, who tried to earn their living on mission by use of their own craft skills. Some missionaries went to the West Indies in 1732; another went to Georgia; yet another to Greenland in 1733. Their mission work was often very fruitful, notably among the indigenous peoples of North America. In 1736, a Moravian missionary named Friedrich Martin arrived in the Caribbean with a desire to minister to the slaves, who had been cruelly brought there from Africa. He wrote in his diary, 'I spoke with a mulatto woman who is very accomplished in the teachings of God. Her name is Rebecca'. Martin eventually married Rebecca (Protten), herself a former slave. She helped establish the first black African Protestant Church in the New World. Despite determined opposition from sugar planters, she brought the Gospel to hundreds of slaves as she faithfully pursued an itinerant evangelistic ministry. It has been said that spiritual revival under Rebecca Protten's ministry contributed significantly to the creation of 'Black Christianity' in the New World [5].

Significantly, the ethos of Zinzendorf and the Moravians might best be summarised from their hymns and songs. For example, Zinzendorf wrote:

Jesu, Thy blood and righteousness
My beauty are, my glorious dress;
Midst flaming worlds, in these arrayed,
With joy shall I lift up my head.

Lord, I believe Thy precious blood
Which at the mercy-seat of God,
For ever doth for sinners plead,
For me, even for my soul was shed.

Lord, I believe, were sinners more
Than sands upon the ocean floor,
Thou hast for all a ransom paid,
For all a full atonement made.

Thou God of power, Thou God of love,
Let the whole world Thy mercy prove!
Now let Thy word o'er all prevail;
Now take the spoils of death and hell.

And who translated this hymn from German into English? John Wesley!

The Methodist Revival in the Eighteenth Century

John Wesley was born in 1703 in Epworth Rectory in England – his father being the local Anglican parish priest. He was the 15th of 19 children (though some of them died very young). His mother Susanna was a devout and serious-minded Christian who prayed with her children in a disciplined and daily pattern. She also provided them with a remarkably full early education: they were all (girls included) taught to read as soon as they could walk and talk. In 1709 the rectory was burned down – possibly by antagonistic parishioners. Young John was rescued from an upstairs window: in later life he often referred to himself as "a brand plucked from the burning" (cf. Zechariah 3: 2, AV) – providentially saved and set apart for God's service. Both John and his brother Charles became students at

Oxford University, and there Charles started a small Christian group for prayer and Bible study, of which brother John became leader. The young George Whitfield was a member of this group. It was nicknamed 'the Holy Club', but as they became deeply involved in devoted, disciplined service to the poor and sick and in the local prison, their fellow-students mockingly called them 'Methodists'.

After ordination as an Anglican priest in 1728, John became a member of the Society for Promoting Christian Knowledge. In 1735, he went with the SPCK as a missionary to Georgia in North America. "Our end in leaving our native country," wrote John, "was not to avoid want, nor to gain riches and honour but singly this – to save our souls; to live wholly to the glory of God." On the journey out to North America, in a furious storm at sea, he noted that his fellow Moravian missionaries had a peace and assurance about them which he did not possess. He was also impressed in general by their holiness of life and their emphasis on personal religious experience. Their demeanour also showed him his own lack of real trust in God and especially his want of assurance of salvation. In fact, John did not have much success with the indigenous Indians or with the European settlers. After 2 years he returned home steadily disturbed by a sense that he himself did not have a full saving faith. "I went to America to convert the Indians … but who will convert me?"

Assurance

On 17th May 1738, John's brother Charles was converted as he read Martin Luther's commentary on Galatians. "I now found myself at peace with God," he wrote, "and rejoiced in the hope of loving Christ". A week later, on 24 May 1738, John's diary graphically describes the radical change which happened to him too: "In the evening I went very unwillingly to a society in Aldersgate Street, where one was reading Luther's preface to the epistle to the Romans. About a quarter before nine, while he was describing the change which God works in the heart through faith in Christ, I felt my heart strangely warmed. I felt I did trust in Christ, Christ alone, for my salvation; and an assurance was given me that He had taken away my sins, even mine, and saved me from the law of sin and death."

This transformational event in John Wesley's life has generally been described by his biographers as his moment of conversion. Though there is surely no need to question the use of the word 'conversion', it is worth further considering Wesley's own description of the event, as quoted above. He clearly lays emphasis on the word 'assurance'. He implies that he was already well aware of those basic scriptural doctrines which are specially treasured by Protestants, but he now became personally assured of them. Whilst most of his biographers have concentrated on the memorable description of the 'heart strangely warmed', perhaps 'assurance' is the more significant reference in Wesley's Journal, for several reasons. First, it relates to a key issue for the early Protestants, as has been recorded in the Coda to Chapter Four in this present book. In this context, it may be relevant that both Wesley's grandparents were of Dissenting stock [6]. The Dissenters overlapped with the Puritan Protestants of an earlier era – the very people in Britain who took the distinctive doctrines of the Reformation most seriously. It is worth noting the dying words of father Samuel Wesley to his son John: "The inner witness, my son, that is what counts; the inner witness". The father's implicit reference was to Romans 8: 16, which concerns the issue of assurance within our own spirits as the Holy Spirit bears witness. Indeed, through the centuries, this text has often been used in referencing the gift of assurance as recorded in the New Testament. Wesley clearly took his father's dying words to heart. Commenting on this deathbed scene, the Reverend Skevington-Wood (one of John Wesley's many biographers) reflects on Samuel's dying comments to his son, "Those words hark back to a typical Puritan emphasis, and also look forward to John Wesley's teaching on assurance" [7].

A second reason for focusing on the word assurance in Wesley's experience of conversion is that this tectonic change in Wesley's life occurred when Luther's Preface to the Epistle to the Romans was being read aloud. Wesley clearly states that the change occurred personally, in his own heart, when Luther was describing in general terms the change of heart which faith brings with it. Therefore, the Wesley brothers – perhaps sub-consciously – were 'tapping in' to a recurrent and basic preoccupation of Protestant experience, from its very beginnings in Luther's own spiritual struggles: the connection between faith and assurance. Indeed, it would have been surprising if the Wesley brothers' own father – and especially their mother – had not emphasized the intimate relationship between faith and assurance which was such a key issue amongst British Dissenters and Puritans alike.

Third, Wesley's use of the word 'assurance' in describing what happened on 24 May 1738 helps to explain his own subsequent understandings of this event. Over the years, as Wesley re-visited that memorable night of 24 May 1738, his own apprecition of the event changed, and even fluctuated. But if the key to his experience lies in the word 'assurance', such changes are to be expected. By its nature, assurance involves a deeply personal, intimate response; and this response, necessarily, involves a significant emotional element. Therefore, a person's perception of their own personal assurance will inevitably change over their later years of developing spiritual experience and maturing emotions.

Whatever, his closest friends and relatives had no difficulty in recognizing that on the evening of 24 May, a crucial change had occurred in Wesley's life, heart and spirit. For example, his brother Charles had no doubts in identifying with what had happened in John's fundamental spiritual situation, having just experienced something similar in his own life. On Tuesday morning, 23 May 1738, Charles (already a writer of hymns) notes: "At nine I began a hymn upon my conversion." The following day, towards ten in the evening, "my brother was brought in triumph by a troop of our friends, and declared, 'I believe.' We sang the hymn with great joy, and parted with prayer." Charles' hymn includes these verses:

> Where shall my wondering soul begin?
> How shall I all to heaven aspire?
> A slave redeemed from death and sin,
> A brand plucked from eternal fire,
> How shall I equal triumphs raise,
> Or sing my great Deliverer's praise?

O how shall I the goodness tell,
Father, which Thou to me hast showed?
That I, a child of wrath and hell,
I should be called a child of God,
Should know, should feel my sins forgiven,
Blest with this antepast of heaven!

Herrnhut

The person who, perhaps more than any other, influenced the Wesley brothers throughout the year 1738 was a young Moravian preacher called Peter Bohler. It was he who had counselled both Charles and John in the early months of 1738, and pointed them towards a conversion experience. He told Wesley, "Preach faith <u>till</u> you have it; and then, <u>because</u> you have it, you <u>will</u> preach faith". Bohler memorably commented to Charles: "If I had a thousand tongues, I would praise Jesus with every one of them". This surely prompted Charles to write, soon after the conversion experiences of both himself and his brother, a hymn which was to become one of his most famous. It begins:

O for a thousand tongues to sing
My dear Redeemer's praise,
The glories of my God and King,
The triumphs of His grace! [8]

Bohler was in conversation with the Wesley brothers only a decade after the unforgettable, transformative experience in Herrnhut of 'the Moravian Pentecost'. Therefore, it is natural to understand that the 'thousand tongues' is related to the gift of 'glossolalia'; and that Charles Wesley was aware of the story of this 'baptism in the Holy Spirit' which the Moravians had then experienced. Unsurprisingly, therefore, the first thing John Wesley did after his conversion was to visit the Moravians in Germany: he spent June to September 1738 with them, greatly benefitting from their fellowship.

'Baptism in the Holy Spirit'

Back in England, the Wesley brothers attended a turn-of-the-year lovefeast and prayertime on I January 1739, joining about sixty of their Moravian friends. George Whitfield was among those present. This turned out to be a pivotal moment in the life-story of John Wesley. He memorably records the occasion in his Journal: "About three in the morning, as we were continuing in prayer, the power of God came mightily upon us, insomuch that many cried out for exceeding joy, and many fell to the ground. As soon as we were recovered a little from that awe and amazement at the presence of his majesty we broke out with one voice, 'We praise Thee, O God; we acknowledge Thee to be the Lord'". This experience may be understood as the real beginning of the Methodist revival in the land. Moravian historians have referred to it as the moment of 'baptism in the Spirit' for the assembled group. [9] Others would describe it as 'John Wesley's personal Pentecost'. As already noted, John was preaching faith in Christ alone before 24 May 1738. He continued to do so during the remainder of that year, after his conversion experience. But from 1st January 1739, several crucial changes occurred in his life and ministry.

A first change was that Wesley accepted George Whitfield's invitation to go to Bristol, to the rough, tough and poor coal-miners working there on the outskirts of the city, and to preach the Gospel to them in the open air. Whitfield had been doing so assiduously since the beginning of 1739: in fact, it would seem that Whitfield had also experienced change in his own life through those meetings in the first days of that year. Concerning those meetings, for example, Whitefield speaks of "a great pouring out of the Spirit among the brethren".[10] From the first months of 1739, Whitfield's ministry focused predominantly on evangelistic preaching in the open-air. This was, in any case, necessary in the case of the Bristol miners. Church buildings were not easily accessible to them; end even if buildings had been available, the grime and coal-dust of their slum conditions would have inhibited their attendance. Wesley agreed to join Whitefield in Bristol, but the concept of open-air preaching was more difficult for him to accept than it had been for Whitfield. On Saturday 31 March 1739, he honestly recorded his reactions: "I could scarce reconcile myself at first to this strange way of preaching in the fields … having been all my life (till very lately) so tenacious of every point relating to decency and order, that I should have thought the saving of souls almost a sin if it had not been done in a church." Perhaps his phrase 'till very lately' obliquely refers to the change that began in him on the first night of the New Year! However, he finally accepted the new challenge of speaking in the open-air. On Monday 2 April, he writes, "I submitted to be more vile, and proclaimed in the highways the glad tidings of salvation, speaking from a little eminence in a ground adjoining to the city, to about three thousand people. The scripture on which I spoke was 'The Spirit of the Lord is upon me, because he hath anointed me to preach the gospel to the poor'". This was an interesting choice of text, following the 1st January experience! The huge significance of starting to preach in the open air was perhaps not fully appreciated even by Whitfield and Wesley themselves at that time. But, in retrospect, it can be seen that from early 1739 onwards, the ministry of both was largely conducted in the open air. Moreover, if you once step outside church buildings, and go where the need to preach the Gospel is greatest, you will surely be led step by step to the ends of the earth! Indeed, the world will become your parish. This is in line with one of Wesley's most memorable comments: "The world is my parish".

A second notable change in Wesley's ministry after 1 January 1739 was the increasingly large crowds who were drawn to hear his preaching and respond to it. For example, on Sunday 29 April, he notes how, in Bristol, he began in the morning by preaching to about 4,000 people; then at Hanham Mount, where about 3,000 were present. In the afternoon he preached at Clifton (no estimate of the numbers there), followed by 7,000 people at Rose Green. In other words, in one day, at least 14,000 people had heard the Gospel! Clearly also – and crucially – an increasing proportion of the listeners were converted through Wesley's powerful preaching. In among all this evangelistic activity, John Wesley himself felt new power and strength. On that same Sunday, 29 April 1739, he records at the end of the day, "Oh how God has renewed my strength! who used ten years ago to be so faint and weary with preaching <u>twice</u> in one day!"

Wesley, 'gifts of administration' [11] and his doctrinal teaching

From this point on, Wesley was constantly travelling and preaching throughout England and Wales. His base cities were London, Bristol and Newcastle. They formed a sort of triangle which included much of England – and he steadily journeyed between them until he was well into his eighties. During his lifetime, he travelled around 250,000 miles, preaching more than 44,000 sermons (an average of just over two every day!). He preached to large numbers at a time – possibly, on occasions, to crowds of over thirty thousand people! Several fundamental points concerning Wesley's ministry and teaching need to be noted.

First, Wesley was a gifted organiser. Even before his conversion, he had recognised the spiritual importance of gathering earnest believers together in small groups; the Holy Club, during his time in Oxford, was the first example. As the Methodist movement grew after 1738, Wesley developed a strong and disciplined infrastructure. Each gathering of newly-converted 'Methodists' in a local area, Wesley called a 'Society'. These Societies, sub-divided into small groups and usually meeting in the middle of the week, were known as 'Classes' and 'Bands'. As the Methodist movement grew, a number of Societies, in the same geographical area, were joined together in order to provide for their pastoral, preaching and administrative needs. Each grouping was 'serviced' by full-time helpers. Those local-area groupings of Societies later became known as 'Circuits'. Finally, Wesley integrated all this intricate organisational infrastructure into an annual nationwide Conference, bringing together all his main friends, helpers and Methodist leaders for prayer, discussion and decision-making. Through Wesley's administrative ability, this organisation provided cohesion for the fastest-growing Protestant movement that England had ever known. By contrast, George Whitfield once said that his own converts, never organised into cohesive groupings like Wesley's Methodists, were 'a rope of sand'. Some have said that Whitfield was a more powerful preacher than Wesley; but Wesley's gift of administration meant his converts were held together in small groups. These groups also provided a base for further evangelism.

Second, Wesley developed Protestant doctrine. He was an Arminian, not a Calvinist, and this led to a sad separation between him and George Whitfield. Wesley believed that God in His grace had restored free-will to lost humanity, and therefore believers could exercise choice regarding faith and salvation. Moreover, this theological stance logically led him to the conclusion that believers who were unrepentant and deliberately continued sinning could lose their salvation.

Third, from Scripture, Wesley developed distinctive, significant and transformative teachings which deeply shaped Methodism and the many individuals and institutions touched by Methodism over the succeeding three centuries [12]. These distinctive teachings can be encapsulated in the phrase "scriptural holiness and social righteousness". As regards scriptural holiness, Wesley developed what was possibly his most striking – and most controversial – teaching: that Christians could expect to be free from every conscious sin in thought, word and deed. This holiness or 'Christian Perfection' was a result of God's grace, so at work in our hearts that we may come to a place where we are totally committed to Jesus, and there is no room for sin in our hearts. This longing is deeply expressed in many of Charles Wesley's hymns:

> My God! I know, I feel Thee mine,
> And will not quit my claim,
> Till all I have is lost in Thine
> And all renewed I am.

Debate continues about Wesley's teaching on this important subject, as to whether our hearts in this life can be fully emptied of sin. Some have suggested that Wesley's understandings on this subject would have been less open to misinterpretation if he had used only descriptions taken from the vocabulary of the New Testament itself [12]. For example, "perfect love" is the descriptive phrase used in I John 4: 18, NRSV. In the 20th Century, a helpful reassessment of Wesley's teaching about holiness and Christian perfection was undertaken by the British Methodist leader the Revd. Dr. W.E. Sangster, in his book <u>The Path to Perfection</u>. [13]

In John Wesley's thinking, social righteousness naturally resulted from scriptural holiness. From earliest days in Oxford, John had emphasized the need to care for widows and orphans, the poor and the sick, prisoners, strangers and the dying. This imperative never left him. The day before he died, in his eighties, he was planning to take some warm clothing to a group of poor folk in central London. He emphasized the practical rule: "Gain all you can, save all you can, give all you can". "Do as much good as you can for as many people as you can as often as you can" was a typical remark. In his Classes everybody was to give a penny a week for the poor. Education and medicine held a particular interest for Wesley. However, his last letter was to William Wilberforce, encouraging him to continue the campaign to abolish the slave trade. It is said that when he died, there was only one item for the government revenue inspectors to check: one silver teaspoon!

The prevenient ('coming before or preceding') work of the Holy Spirit was crucial to spreading the Good News of Jesus in all Wesley's understanding of evangelism. The Spirit goes before us, prepares the way, and is active in the world. Particularly in the early years of revival, many dramatic events took place, especially as individuals were convicted by the gospel message (though not all of those manifestations were endorsed by Wesley himself). These events reflected some of the descriptions of the Holy Spirit's activities as recorded in the Book of Acts. Charles' hymns, again, frequently take up his elder brother's theme of the prevenient work of the Spirit:

> Come, Holy Ghost, for Thee I call,
> Spirit of burning come! …
>
> Refining Fire, go through my heart,
> Illuminate my soul;
> Scatter Thy life through every part,
> And sanctify the whole.

During the 19th Century a popular summary was developed of Methodist teaching and preaching from the preceding century. This tabulated synopsis became widely used within Methodist circles, partly because it memorably encapsulated the distinctives of Wesley's teaching and practice. Often referred to as the "Four Alls of Methodism," it would be an anachronism to think they were in place in their later form from the beginnings of the Methodist movement in the 18th Century. Even so, they do memorably express those Methodist emphases which were evident from 1738 onwards, as fully demonstrated in the sermons of John Wesley and the hymns of brother Charles:

1. All need to be saved:
    "O for a trumpet voice on all the world to call ..."

2. All can be saved:
    "For all, for all my Saviour died".

3. All can know they are saved:
    "My God I know, I feel Thee mine ..."

4. All can be saved to the uttermost:
    "Perfectly restored in Thee".

Even so, it might be said that Wesley's ultimate concern was more with the character of the Methodist people than their creed. Wesley's own description of the character of a Methodist was succinct. A Methodist is a person who is experiencing that: "God has poured out His love into our hearts by the Holy Spirit, whom He has given us" (Romans 5: 5, NIV).

One other distinctive feature, which marked out the character of Wesley's Methodists, was the use of lay leaders in the Societies. This was to become a hallmark of the Methodist movement. From the beginning, Class leaders and Society leaders were generally layfolk, not ordained presbyters. This was at the time a matter of practical necessity – there were no ordained priests available. The few presbyters who joined the Methodist movement - like John's brother Charles and the saintly Fletcher of Madeley – were too few in number to provide adequate local oversight. In any case, only a few of this small group were free to itinerate round the country as Wesley did. It took John a long time – and a radical change of heart – to think of unordained people leading worship and preaching. In many of his attitudes he was still naturally a 'High Churchman'. But in the end – partly through strong advice from his mother Susanna – John accepted this 'novel practice'. So it was that practical demands required Wesley to begin to use lay preachers and lay pastoral overseers.

One final characteristic of the early Methodists requires mention. It has already been noted that as a younger man, Wesley had affirmed, "The world is my parish". By the end of his life, he and his closest associates focussed more and more on the need to take the Good News to the ends of the earth. Wesley, too old to leave Britain himself, encouraged other Methodist preachers and leaders to do so: for example, Francis Asbury to North America and Thomas Coke yearning to go to India. (Wesley's 'ordination' of Thomas Coke in 1784, for mission beyond the shores of Britain, was a decisive moment in the development of the Methodist movement.) By this time, however, the British Methodists were by no means alone in being stirred by a global missionary vision. Many others not directly associated with the Methodist movement had also started to grapple with the imperative from Jesus Himself that His followers should commit themselves to world-wide mission.

NOTES AND REFERENCES

"God has poured His love into our hearts by the Holy Spirit, whom He has given us" (Romans 5. 5, NIV), at the heart of this chapter's title, summarizes both Moravian and Methodist emphases concerning the character of a disciple of Jesus.

1   Woodbridge and James, op. cit., p.458
2   Gonzalez, op. cit., p. 263
3   Some of this detail is draw from Liarden, R., God's Generals; the Revivalists (Whitaker House, New Kensington, PA, USA, 2008) IBSN: 978 – 1 – 60374 – 095 – 1 ps. 15 - 17
4   Woodbridge and James, op. cit., p.457
5   Ibid., p.459
6   Ibid., p.406
7   Skevington-Wood, A., The Burning Heart, John Wesley: Evangelist (The Paternoster Press, UK, 1967) p. 27
8   See Telford, J., The New Methodist Hymn Book Illustrated in History and Experience (Epworth Press, London, 1934 – Third Edition November 1941), ps. 1 – 4. Telford suggests that the hymn was probably written about 21 May 1739. He further notes: 'Its premier place in the Wesleyan hymn-book since 1780 has given it a hold on universal Methodism such as scarcely any other hymn possesses. It is also the first hymn in The Methodist Hymnal (1905) of America'. Telford quotes a comment by a Mr. Stead: 'Given the first place in the Methodist hymn-book, it may be said to strike the key-note of the whole of Methodism' – globally!
9   See, for example, https//www.evanwiggs.com/revival/history/moravian.html: 'the baptism in the Holy Spirit upon the Moravians and then the Methodists, produced a flood of sacred songs.'
10   George Whitefield's Journals (The Banner of Truth Trust, 1960) p. 198
11   1 Corinthians 12: 28, NIV
12   The present writer is extremely grateful for Teaching Notes provided by the Revd. Dr. Peter Ensor on the subject of Wesley's doctrinal understandings. These notes were used in Dr. Ensor's lecturing to the Theology Department of Kenya Methodist University in the years before 2015 and after 2017. The course was entitled 'Wesley and Methodism'.
13   Sangster, W. E., The Path to Perfection: An Examination and Restatement of John Wesley's Doctrine of Christian Perfection (Hodder and Stoughton, 1943). Between 1939 and 1955, Dr. Sangster was the Superintendent Minister

of Westminster Central Hall, which occupies a prominent position in central London, opposite the Houses of Parliament. He also became a President of the British Methodist Conference.

AFRICAN PERSPECTIVES: SOME DISCUSSION POINTS

1   Consider Wesley's experience at the Aldersgate Meeting on 24 May 1738. On the one hand, it has generally been described as the moment of Wesley's conversion. On the other hand, it included a journey which began many years earlier. Moreover, in the years after 1738, his own understandings of the event were modified. Reflect on Wesley's conversion experience in the light of your own. Would you describe your own experience of coming to faith in Jesus as 'sudden' or 'gradual'. What importance would you attach in your own spiritual journey to the element of 'assurance'.

2   How would you understand the experience of John Wesley and his friends on Ist January 1739 at the Moravian all-night Prayer Time? Would you describe it as a 'baptism in the Holy Spirit'? How does 'baptism in the Holy Spirit' relate to Pentecostal experience and Christian growth in sub-Saharan Africa since the early 1900s?

3   Wesley was a gifted organiser and administrator. What importance would you attach to those gifts in the context of the pentecostal movement sweeping sub-Saharan Africa, South America, and South-East Asia in the first years of the Third Millennium?

CHAPTER SIX

"TO THE ENDS OF THE EARTH" 19TH CENTURY WORLDWIDE MISSION FROM EUROPE

"Repentance and forgiveness of sins . . .
proclaimed in His Name to all nations"

Introduction

From the end of the 18th Century onwards, there was a huge expansion of Protestant Christian mission from Europe to the rest of the globe. This expansion was largely undertaken by English-speaking white Europeans: it has been estimated that 80% of non-Roman Catholic missionaries from the late 18th to the late 20th Centuries were from the English-speaking world. From the middle of the 19th Century onwards, a steadily-increasing proportion of those white missionaries came from the USA rather than from Europe. This chapter presents just three examples of this 'missionary explosion', and its impact in three different continents.

William Carey (1761 – 1834) and India

Mainly a self-taught man with little formal education, William Carey was in his early years both the village cobbler and the pastor of the local Baptist Church. Visitors to his home or his shop would note that there was always a book at his elbow! "Attempt great things for God; expect great things from God", became his memorable motto. His studies convinced him that God's desire was to see 'the heathen' converted to Christ, and from 1792 onwards this became the passion of his life. He faced much opposition from older Baptist leaders, with their fairly extreme Calvinist understandings. On one occasion, whilst he was speaking in a meeting, he was famously told, 'Sit down, young man'. God would convert the heathen in His own time and by His own methods: 'He does not need our help!' But Carey pursued his vision. May 1792 found him preaching on Isaiah 54: 2–3, "Lengthen thy cords and strengthen thy stakes". Four months later, the Baptist Missionary Society was formed, and in June 1793, Carey left with his family for India – the Society's first missionary – arriving in India in the November of that year.

The British East India Company was very suspicious of missionaries, and after a while, Carey withdrew into the interior, where the Company's writ did not run so large. There, his wife became more and more mentally ill, causing his children to grow up as undisciplined ragamuffins. Yet within five years, Carey had translated the Scriptures into Bengali. He had an amazing gift for languages, but was untrained in translation work, so his failure to understand usage and idiom meant the translation was virtually incomprehensible. With great courage and patience, he had to start the work all over again! In 1799, a schoolmaster and a printer arrived from the Baptist Missionary Society, and they encouraged Carey to move to the tiny Danish colony of Serampore: the Danes did not share the anti-mission attitude of the British East India Company. The new printer, Ward, was chosen as the pastor of the new congregation, and in partnership with Carey the trio became extraordinarily productive.

Carey seemed independent and far-sighted (though perhaps in the main he was applying the teaching and example he found in the New Testament) in relation to spreading the Gospel. He saw Christian mission as five-pronged, with equal attention being needed for each element. First and foremost came the widespread preaching of the Gospel. Preaching tours were organized far afield from Serampore, up the Ganges, into Orissa, and as far away as Burma. Second, great attention should be given to the translation and distribution of the Scriptures, the written Word of God.

This translation and distribution work was seen as the best possible way of supporting the preaching. In thirty years, the trio of Ward, Marshman (the schoolmaster) and Carey made six whole translations of the Bible into different languages; twenty-three complete New Testaments; and some Bible portions in ten other languages. Thus a total of thirty-nine languages were touched in thirty years! The third 'prong' of Carey's understanding of Christian mission was the establishment of a local church straight away (in the Twenty-First Century, the term "church planting" would describe the activity). When further converts were made, they could then be baptized into an existing church congregation, already settled and planted on Indian soil. Because the Baptists in England were far away, they could not control the new church. So this proved a better way of organizing Christian mission, with the focus on an indigenously-rooted local church. Fourth, effective mission required a profound study of the cultural background and thought-forms of the local non-Christian peoples. There was no idea of compromising the uniqueness of Jesus and the exclusive claims of faith in Him; they understood other religions as the delusions of the devil. 'Yet they saw clearly that the missionary must understand not only the language but also the thought-world of those to whom the Gospel is to be preached'[1]. Fifthly, for Carey, an enduring Christian Church meant the training at the earliest possible moment of an indigenous ministry team (a priority much neglected by many other mainline Protestant missionary societies). Carey wrote in 1805: "another part of our work is the forming of our native brethren to usefulness, fostering every kind of genius, and cherishing every gift and grace in them . . . It is only by means of native preachers we can hope for the universal spread of the Gospel through this immense continent" [2]. Though 21st Century church historians might not use the same vocabulary as Carey, they would largely endorse Carey's approach to worldwide Christian mission. Thus, he is not only understood as the 'father of modern missions', but he also exemplifies what would now be considered 'best practice' in the application of missionary zeal.

American Camp Meetings, British Primitive Methodism, and the African Niger Delta

Some elements in the 19th Century missionary 'explosion' were by no means a simple matter of British missionaries heading off from Europe to the other continents of the world. The establishment of Primitive Methodist 'Overseas Missions' gives an insight into the kind of chronological and spiritual complexities which could sometimes arise. In the early years of the 19th Century, the main Methodist grouping became known as 'Wesleyan Methodists'. A number of 'splinter groups' broke away from this main Methodist grouping, the largest and most significant of the splinter groups becoming known as 'Primitive Methodists'. The emergence of Primitive Methodism is instructive concerning the development of world-wide Christian mission.

It has been recorded in Chapter 4 how 'Holy Fairs', established in Central and South-West Scotland, had spread to the American colonies in the late 17th Century. There, they evolved from 'Holy Fairs' to 'Camp Communions', and thence to 'Camp Meetings'. Towards the end of the 18th Century, one well-known preacher in America who used camp meetings was Lorenzo 'Crazy' Dow (1777 – 1834)[3]. Eccentric and theatrical in his behaviour, he became an important figure in the American 'Second Great Awakening'. It was said that he addressed more people than any other preacher of his era. Apart from the Bible, at one time his autobiography was the best-selling book in the USA. He became a Methodist Circuit Preacher in 1798, and stayed essentially Methodist in doctrine all his life. In 1799, he visited England, and powerfully influenced Hugh Bourne (1777 – 1852) who became convinced of the efficacy of camp meetings. What were camp meetings? They were large gatherings of earnest Christians coming together for a full day, a whole weekend, or, on occasions, for extended weekends. The Camp Meetings usually took place in the countryside, and attendees brought their own provisions and improvised camping equipment. They focused on communal prayer, together with revival addresses. Believers were built up – often into deeper consecration to Christ – and those who had not truly committed their lives to Christ were often converted.

In 1804, after hearing Wesley's teaching about entire sanctification[24], Bourne experienced his own personal encounter with the Holy Spirit; this has sometimes been described as 'Hugh Bourne's Pentecost'. Three years later, on Sunday 31st May 1807, Bourne organized a camp meeting at Mow Cop, a prominent hill rising from the plains of the West Midlands in England. The meeting started at 8am and continued until 8pm. The national Methodist authorities frowned on both the style and the content of these meetings, and in due course Bourne was forced out of Methodism, having suffered considerable persecution. This constituted the beginning of Primitive Methodism, which was so-called because of Wesley's repeated assertion that Methodism was none other than basic and original (that is, 'primitive') Christianity, validated (as Wesley understood it) by New Testament narratives and teaching. Hugh Bourne himself was a remarkable character. He began life as a simple carpenter. But — entirely self-taught – he acquired a knowledge of Greek, Hebrew, Latin and French! William Clowes (1780 – 1851) became a partner with Bourne in the formation of Primitive Methodism. By the time of Bourne's death in 1852, Primitive Methodism numbered some 110,000 members, with 560 travelling preachers. Bourne has been described as 'tireless in mind and body, eloquent, and astonishingly gifted in literary and organizing ability'.

By the end of the 19th Century, Primitive Methodism had made a distinct contribution to the worldwide 'Missionary Movement' from Europe. In Africa, for example, in 1893, a Primitive Methodist Mission Station was opened at Archibongon in Igboland (part of present-day Eastern Nigeria). In the early years of the 20th Century, a quite exceptional event occurred in Igboland which related closely to the Primitive Methodist Mission there, through the agency of an Igbo preacher named Garrick Sokari Braide (c.1882 – 1918). He experienced a personal outpouring of spiritual power which resulted in mass evangelism in the Niger Delta. Braide's ministry has been estimated to have reached over 1,000,000 people, in an area where previously the numerical growth of Christianity under European missionaries had been very slow. Braide came from Igboland, and when news of his work in the Delta reached Igboland, large numbers of Igbo people turned to Christ. Most significantly from the perspective of this study, Braide directed converts in Igboland to the Primitive Methodist

Mission, which thus benefitted enormously, with multiples of thousands becoming members of the Mission's Churches [5].

It has been suggested that Braide provided the African prototype for other indigenous Christian leaders who were used in African 20th Century revivals. Like Braide, they were often given the title 'Prophet.' Braide therefore assumes a particular significance in 20th Century African Church History in general. However, the more focussed point to be made here is this: Why was it that Primitive Methodism particularly benefitted from Prophet Braide's work? Was there a resonance between the spirituality of Primitive Methodism and Braide's evangelism? Was the ethos of the Primitive Methodist camp meeting particularly fitting for evangelism in Igboland? However these questions may be answered, one striking piece of circumstantial evidence may be offered towards establishing the reality of the inter-continental connections outlined in this section. It came from the lips of a 21st Century Igbo Methodist leader. When he visited the Primitive Methodist Museum in Northern England, he spontaneously commented that he felt he had 'come home'!

James Hudson-Taylor (1832 – 1905) and the China Inland Mission

Hudson Taylor's mission to China represents a rather later mission than that of Carey's to India.. William Carey was a pioneer of the 19th Century European Missionary movement: he lived out a global missionary attitude. The great significance of Hudson-Taylor was in the novel evangelistic methods he used in gaining access to a non-European culture, and in the vast impact of his China Inland Mission on the most populous country on earth.

Hudson Taylor came to Christ as a sixteen-year-old, and not many months after his conversion, he noted how "in unreserved consecration I put myself, my life, my friends, my all, upon the altar … Within a few months of this time of consecration, the impression was wrought into my soul that it was in China the Lord wanted me" [6]. Before long, he learned this crucial truth: "From day to day and from hour to hour, to live as men who wait for the Lord; that thus living it was immaterial, so to speak, whether He should or should not come at any particular hour, the important thing being to be so ready for Him as to be able, whenever He might appear, to give an account of one's stewardship with joy, and not with grief" [7].

He studied medicine in London, as a preparation for going as a missionary to China. He made best use of every opportunity to share the Good News of Jesus. After bursting into tears over one patient who seemed unwilling to listen, the man allowed him to speak and pray with him. "I have often thought since," wrote Taylor, "in connection with this case and the work of God generally, of the words, 'He that goes forth weeping, bearing precious seed, shall doubtless come again rejoicing, bringing his sheaves with him.' Perhaps if there were more of that intense distress for souls that leads to tears, we should more frequently see the results we desire. Sometimes it may be that while we are complaining of the hardness of the hearts of those we are seeking to benefit, the hardness of our own hearts, and our own feeble apprehension of the solemn reality of eternal things, may be the true cause of our want of success" [8]. Taylor went to China at the age of twenty-one. Within seven years he had not only married and learnt Chinese, he had also adopted Chinese dress and the pigtail as the most obvious ways of identifying with the Chinese people. Moreover, he had resigned from the Chinese Evangelization Society, being led to depend on God for everything. 'God's work, done in God's way, will never lack God's resources', was Hudson-Taylor's memorable summary of his position. His behaviour and standards provoked fierce, even fanatical, opposition among some of the other European missionaries around him. In 1860 he returned to England in very poor health.

However, in 1865, without recognition and without denominational support, he returned to China and, single-handed, founded the China Inland Mission (CIM). This Mission, for a time, was the largest Protestant mission in the world. Taylor once said, "The sun never rose over China but what it found me on my knees". His mission principles were very different from those in operation in other missions and missionary-churches in the Protestant world at this time. First, the CIM was interdenominational. Only later, in Edinburgh in 1910, did many other British Missionary Societies begin to recognize the value of ecumenical Christian mission. Taylor's

Mission was conservative in theology, but would accept as missionaries any who would sign its simple doctrinal statement. Second, formal education was not a prerequisite for acceptance by the CIM. Furthermore, thirdly, the direction of the Mission would be in China, not from England. He himself, based in China, provided the rapid decision-making and flexible administration which were vital in a dynamically growing mission-field. More radically still, in a fourth new concept, Hudson-Taylor insisted on CIM missionaries acculturating, to identify themselves as far as possible with the Chinese people – wearing Chinese dress was an obvious first step. Finally, the overriding aim of the mission was ever-widening evangelism. Pastoring, education, and medical work could be undertaken, but nothing was to obscure or hinder the central focus of winning folk for Christ. Nothing was to cut across that fundamental concern for evangelism.

Hudson Taylor faced many difficulties: he experienced ill-health, and also the death of his beloved wife in 1870. Other European missionaries (and their churches at home) failed to understand his approach. Moreover, difficulties arose through being misunderstood by the Chinese authorities, sometimes leading to life-threatening situations. Yet the China Inland Mission experienced astounding success. In 1865, no Protestant missionary had ever been seen in eleven of China's eighteen Provinces. By 1882, especially through the work of the CIM, all the provinces had been visited, with Christian missionaries in all but three of them. By 1895, CIM had six hundred and forty-one missionaries, drawn from many different lands, working in China – some of them in the far west of that great country, some in Sinkiang (Chinese Turkestan) and others on the borders of Tibet. In 1879, David Hill (a Methodist) led to Christ a Chinese Confucian scholar, Pastor His. He worked with D.E. Hoste, one of the most prayerful missionaries in CIM, as a colleague. This led to ten years of fruitful cooperation. Then even greater public notice was taken of the CIM when it was joined by 'the Cambridge Seven' – a group of University graduates which included CT Studd, an England national cricketer. Studd went on to found Worldwide Evangelisation for Christ (WEC). Not everyone agreed with Hudson Taylor and his methods. But no one could seriously challenge the undoubted fruitfulness of CIM work. And no one could easily remain unmoved by accounts of the mobility, simplicity and devotion of the CIM missionaries. Moreover, well into the 21ˢᵗ Century, Chinese Christians were still visiting Hudson-Taylor's birthplace in Britain as a mark of respectful pilgrimage, recognizing the long-term impact of his ministry on the globe's most populous nation.

NOTES AND REFERENCES

"Repentance and forgiveness of sins . . . proclaimed in His Name to all nations" in the chapter sub-title is the NRSV translation of Luke 24: 47.

[1] Neill, Stephen, A History of Christian Missions (Penguin Books, London, 1964) p.261

[2] Ibid., p. 264 – 265

[3] Milburn, Geoffrey, Primitive Methodism (Epworth Press, Peterborough, UK, 2002) ISBN 0 – 7162 – 05548, p. 5 offers more insights into the character of Dow's ministry

[4] 'Entire sanctification' is another term for describing Wesley's doctrine of Christian Perfection

[5] Ekebusi, C., The Life and Ministry of Prophet Garrick Sokari Braide: Elijah the Second of Niger Delta, Nigeria (c.1882 – 1918) (Peter Lang, Bern, Switzerland, 2015) ISBN 978 – 3 – 0343 – 1878 - 5. The Revd Dr Ekebusi provides a wealth of valuable new material, which has relevance for the whole of 20th Century African Church History. Dr Ekebusi handles his research material competently and sensitively, being himself Igbo by heritage, and an active Methodist Minister

[6] Taylor, Hudson, Hudson Taylor's 'Retrospect' (Overseas Missionary Fellowship, London, 1974, 18th Edition) ps. 15 – 16

[7] Ibid., p. 19

[8] Ibid., ps. 41 – 42

AFRICAN PERSPECTIVES: SOME DISCUSSION POINTS

1   Note the ways in which Carey and Hudson Taylor were alike in their missionary ministries, and how they were different. Aim to extract from the ministries and methods of both missionaries, points of universal relevance to Christian mission. How do these points apply in present-day Africa?

2   What makes for evangelistic effectiveness? Evaluate the different responses - especially in the methods of European missionaries – to Jesus' command, "Make disciples of all nations".

3   Sokari Braide was the first in a succession of Christian African Prophets. What is your understanding of their significance? Do you know of any Christian 'African Prophet' who worked in your own home area?

CHAPTER SEVEN

CHRISTIAN MISSION IN WEST AFRICA IN THE 19TH AND 20TH CENTURIES

"Ethiopia shall soon stretch out her hands unto God"

Psalm 68 verse 31 became a favourite verse for many African Christians in the 20th Century – for them 'Ethiopia' standing for the whole continent. This present study is narrowed down to concentrate on a meaningful but manageable region: West Africa, where Christian mission is particularly well-documented. But since, spatially, the whole of Europe can be fitted into West Africa, this is not a small region! Moreover, by the beginning of the 21st Century, this region had assumed global significance in the unfolding history of the Christian church. It also provides an example of historical movements which were at work in many other parts of the world as well. Present-day West Africa is experiencing great spiritual growth. But it is also growing in other significant ways as well. For example, it has been estimated that, at present rates of population growth, Nigeria will be the third most populous country in the world before the end of the 21st Century; and it is already the most populous "black" nation on the planet, providing a major contribution to international Christian mission. Moreover, it is a region where, at the beginning of the 21st Century, already Islamists actively present a disruptive extremist presence.

Muslim expansion

During the 18th Century, European military success in many areas of the world had resulted in humiliation for the failing Ottoman and Mughal empires. These empires were Islamic in faith, and, partly in response to perceived political weakness, various Muslim renewal movements sprang up. In West Africa, the mystically-minded Sufi understanding of Islam gave zeal and strength to the pastoralist Fulani people, whose home was the West African savanna grassland between the forested area to the south and the Sahara desert to the north. They established a string of Muslim emirates which replaced previous kingdoms. The instrument of advance was the jihad, aimed at establishing a purer form of Islam. The greatest of these jihads was led by the campaigning Sufi scholar Shehu Usman Dan Fodio. In the early 19th Century, the most plausible picture of the religious future for West Africa was for it to become overwhelmingly Muslim – and, indeed, Muslim growth was spectacular throughout the century [1]. Even into the late 20th Century, the vision of some Muslims was to 'dip the Quran into the Atlantic Ocean': in other words, to see the whole of West Africa being thoroughly Islamized right down to the Atlantic littoral. Yet this Muslim vision did not become a reality. Muslim advance generally petered out around the 10th degree of latitude North. It was not the Sahara desert that provided a barrier to the southward spread of Islam. Very many Muslims were to be found throughout the West African sahel, hundreds of miles south of the desert. The barrier to further Islamization came, in fact, from the south, where a new dynamic Christian mission movement was arising from the opposite direction.

African Catechists

While European Missionary Societies were sending out missionary volunteers from the early 19th Century onwards, a less formal dispersal of Christian knowledge was exuberantly emanating from the British Protestant footholds in the coastal lands of such countries as we now call Sierra Leone, Ghana and Nigeria. Young men from far inland went to find work on the coast; by the time they returned home, some had a new faith in their hearts, and many had new songs on their lips. From the port of Freetown, Sierra Leone, for example, the first Krio settlers – virtually all self-proclaimed Christians – traded not only into their own hinterland, but also eastwards along the coast, until some, together with Yoruba returnee ex-slaves, reached Badagry in present-day Nigeria.

Through the 19ᵗʰ and 20ᵗʰ Centuries, countless numbers of Christian missionaries from Europe and America pursued ministries in West Africa. Most of these white missionaries quickly discovered the vital role of local catechists. These were lay African Christian converts who could speak the Christian Gospel in the African way. They were a combination of local pastor, preacher, teacher and evangelist, and their local voices were better able to convey what the missionaries had been trying to pass on in what was, to African ears, alien cultural forms. The catechists did it with joy and exuberance. 'Africa must be converted by Africans' was a principle illustrated in local situations over and over again.

From the latter part of the 19ᵗʰ Century onwards, missionaries spent much time and effort reducing the local spoken vernaculars into written form – especially in order to translate the Bible into the 'heart-language' of the people. They also laid great emphasis on education, providing the literacy required for their converts to read the Bible in their own tongues. As African peoples read the Scriptures, they picked up themes which the European missionaries themselves did not readily relate to; nor ones which those missionaries ever expected their converts to focus on. For example, the Bible is a Book full of signs and wonders, healings and miracles and much prophecy, all testifying to God's sovereign power (as summarised, for example, in Hebrews 2: 4). These were the sort of evidences that in Africa were used as validations that a person and their teaching was truly from God. The Bible spoke of a world in which spiritual powers were in conflict: this was the world which African people already inhabited and knew. This was not, however, the case in the 'enlightened' rationalistic and 'scientific' world inhabited by the European missionaries. In fact, Africans often took the Book more seriously and more literally than the very missionaries who had risked their lives to bring it to them. Africans confidently waited for concrete and specific results from the God who acts in power, in a way that

Europeans, often imbued with liberal 'biblical criticism', and a mechanistic 'scientific' world-view, did not themselves expect to see!

Possibly the largest single social issue facing African converts was polygamy. As they read the Bible for themselves, they found the question of polygamy could be seen from a rather different perspective than that presented by the white missionaries. African converts were quick to understand that, at least in the Old Testament, polygamy did not present the massive and problematic issue that Europeans seemed to make of it. They also saw (as Luther had seen four centuries before them!) that the New Testament could be read in such a way that polygamy was not specifically forbidden in its pages. If polygamy presented a moral or social dilemma for African converts, the European missionaries themselves were often presented with their own very practical and tangible challenges of a different nature. For example, in much of Africa, especially in the more arid areas, the biggest issue in everyday life was the provision of an adequate water-supply; and adequate water largely depended on adequate annual rainfall. The rain was especially important at the times when it was needed for crops to grow. If traditional rainmakers seemed able to do something about the problem, surely those who brought the Good News of God's care for each detail of life should be able to pray effectively for rain. Prayer about issues such as 'rain-making' was not something that most white Christians, even committed Bible-believing evangelicals, had ever thought of practising!

One unexpected but powerful story concerning the issue of rain comes from the town of Kailahun in the British Sierra Leone Protectorate, near to the border with Liberia and Guinea. Although it is from a later date than the period mainly under discussion in these paragraphs, it beautifully illustrates the whole subject of praying for rain. It is also a well-documented incident. On Tuesday 31 October 1950, during a period of serious local political violence, rumours spread that certain factions were going to burn Kailahun down that night. A good breeze was blowing and the palm-thatch roofs of the mud houses were very dry; for, as was usual by the end of October, the six months of 'dry season' had fully set in. When Pastor Rogers (the local Methodist Catechist and church leader) reported the rumour of serious violence to the Reverend Leslie Wallace (the European missionary in the town), the latter asked how such a disaster could be averted. Pastor Rogers said the only thing to do was to pray for rain, even though it was well into the dry season, when it would <u>never</u> rain! So later that day, five Christians met together and prayed. By eight o'clock in the evening, the town was miraculously saturated by a tropical storm, which not only prevented any possibility of arson, but also literally dampened the excitement of the rioters. Two days later, uniformed police from Freetown arrived to take charge, and by Saturday 4 November, the situation had been stabilised to such a degree that the police were able to engage a town team in a friendly football-match.[2] Where the white missionary had not seen a way forward, the indigenous catechist had exercised his African-oriented inspired Christian faith!

Later in the 20th Century, the Revd Gilbert Hall had powerful, positive memories of another catechist leader, with whom he ministered in north-west Nigeria. This catechist would take a bicycle with paniers full of simple medicines, and pedal to distant villages where the Christian Gospel had never been preached. On arrival at a village, he would sit informally on the roadside and offer simple medical help to passers-by who were in obvious need. Often, this would gain him entrance into the village where, later, in the cool of the early evening, he would preach the Gospel. "He taught me more about Jesus Christ than any other person I'd ever met," recalled the Revd Hall. "He was the perfect example of Jesus Christ"[3].

Missionary Expansion by established European Churches

Henry Venn was a grandson of one of the original 18th Century London-based 'Clapham Sect' members. He became General Secretary of the (evangelical Anglican) Church Missionary Society in 1841, and served in that position for decades. He initiated a 'three-self' principle: the African church was to be self-supporting, self-governing and self-propagating. (Strangely, these principles do not seem vastly different from the similar 'three-self' statements governing the official Christian churches in China during the late 20th and early 21st Centuries!) Samuel Ajayi Crowther (c.1807 – 1892) was a personal friend of Venn. He was a Yoruba man who had been freed from a slave ship by the Royal Navy: he then settled in Sierra Leone. He was consecrated in Canterbury Cathedral in 186 as the first African Anglican bishop.

Crowther was made Bishop of the Niger Delta – jealousy among European missionaries had prevented him from ministry among his own people. In the Delta, he was faced with a ruthless trading company, the Royal Niger Company. Moreover, a younger generation of British missionaries later arrived in the area 'endowed with all the self-confidence of English public schoolboys and the brisk austerity of late Victorian Evangelicalism, plus a dose of plain racism'. [4] One 24-year-old described Crowther (more than 50 years his senior) as 'a charming old man, really guileless and humble … but he certainly does not seem called of God to be an overseer'.

There was growing racial tension between the Sierra Leoneans recruited by Crowther and the British staff who managed the steamer carrying mission members up and down the Niger. Eventually discipline broke down among the Sierra Leoneans, which provided a reason (or perhaps an excuse?) for the younger British missionaries to disband them. Debate continues over this serious incident. Were the young British missionaries expressing a racist attitude when they dismantled the team put together by Bishop Crowther, or were they responding to an urgent moral crisis in the mission? Crowther was persuaded to resign in 1890 (which he did with remarkable grace) and died in 1892.

A separate Lecture would really be needed to concentrate on Catholic mission advance in West Africa during this period. One of the most significant European figures in this advance was Fr. Francis Libermann (1802 – 1852) who became the leader of the Holy Ghost Fathers. Libermann's chief principle in mission was the establishment of an indigenous church, not simply the baptism of as many as possible. The greatest need in this work, as he understood it, was 'to form a native clergy rooted in the country, a native hierarchy'. Together with other Catholic missionary societies, they united into an important mission advance from the Niger Delta, up the Niger and Benue rivers, eventually establishing Catholicism in what is now Northern Nigeria.

African Prophets

William Wade Harris or Prophet Harris (1865 – 1929) was a native Liberian who opposed the mis-government of the Monrovian African-American elite in his up-country tribal area. He wanted the area handed over to the British, to be administered by them. At one time imprisoned as a subversive, Harris was granted Spirit-inspired visions that he should begin a prophetic missionary ministry. By 1914, he was striding through villages in the Ivory Coast and the Gold Coast (present-day Ghana), dressed in a simple white robe. He bore a gourd calabash of water, with a tall cross-staff in one hand and an English family Bible in the other. He preached the coming of Christ and the absolute necessity of destroying all traditional cult objects: "Thou shalt have no other gods before Me." His sincerity and fearlessness could hardly be doubted. He wanted no money, only the repentance of the people, preaching a simple, straightforward message to the ordinary villagers, who flocked to hear him. Crucial to his ministry in worship, healing and deliverance was a team of two or three women singing and playing gourd rattles; this became a distinctive characteristic of the churches Harris planted. Little in Harris' message could be considered alien to the mainstream Christianity he had learnt as an episcopal catechist. In fact, he himself recommended converts to join the Methodists, although problems were later to arise because of his own tolerance of polygamy (though he strongly preached against the sin of adultery).

Harris showed an extraordinary ability to leave behind him settled permanent local churches (a Wesley rather than a Whitfield!). Almost 10 years after Prophet Harris' departure back to Liberia, English missionaries sent by the Methodist Missionary Society to the Ivory Coast found that, though many converts baptised by Harris had fallen away, yet around forty-five thousand people were still waiting for more, after ten years! (This extraordinary story is further considered in Chapter Eight.) These expectant converts were continuing to accept the incomparable importance of the Word of God, and were still awaiting teachers to come with fuller instruction for them, as Harris had himself prophesied. Harris' ministry had surely been conducted with great "power from on high" (Luke 24:

49, NIV). Though the most internationally recognized African Prophet abroad in West Africa at the beginning of the 20th Century, Harris was not alone. Another African prophet (whose ministry in fact preceded Harris) was Garrick Sokari Braide. His work has already been discussed in Chapter Six.

Throughout the 20th Century, in a burgeoning dynamic, African Independent Churches (sometimes described as 'African Indigenous Churches', or 'African-initiated Churches') continued to develop in the sub-Saharan part of the continent. Though they often grew out of 'traditional' European or American 'mainline churches', yet they owed little to the pentecostal movement which was growing exponentially in other continents. As with Braide and Harris' ministries, they were largely African initiatives, engaging with African culture and African spiritual perspectives. They were generally autonomous expressions of Christian faith, honed to the cultural milieu of thousands of ordinary African people. This process is sometimes included within the term 'Africanisation'. The leaders of these Churches were often described as 'Prophets.' Some of the most notable of these prophets – who ministered independently but contemporaneously – were: Simon Kimbangu in the Congo; Zakayo Kivuli in Western Kenya; John Maranke in Zimbabwe; and Isaiah Shembe in South Africa. In fact the largest of these movements was among the Zulu people of South Africa, where prophets and followers called themselves amaSiyoni (Zionists).

One major factor in the growth of these new churches was the terrible worldwide influenza epidemic of 1918. Western medicine (often administered in Christian mission clinics and hospitals) seemed powerless against the virus. So some African Christians turned to their own style of Christian healing ministry, which was validated by the Gospel narratives, and which those brought up in the atmosphere of a traditional African village could better comprehend. In West Africa, these churches were commonly known by the Yoruba word meaning 'owners of prayer': Aladura. Although these churches were prophet-led, they had a serious respect for authority within the church organization, and quickly developed strong hierarchical structures. This respect for authority came partly from

European missionary churches – especially those with a 'High Church' tradition. But it was also from a deeply-rooted African cultural expression of respect for religious and political leaders.

Throughout sub-Saharan Africa during the 20th Century, a great pride in the 'Ethiopian faith' often ran through the 'new churches'. Psalm 68: 31 continued to be a key text for many, together with a somewhat mythologised understanding of the continuity brought to the continent over the centuries by the Christian Church in Ethiopia itself. African churches would bring African solutions to African problems. For example, the constitution of the Aladura churches proclaimed, "Ethiopia or Africa shall raise up her own hands unto the Great Jehovah-God under the Spiritual Guide and lead her own indigenous sons" [5].

Towards the end of the 20th Century and into the beginning of the Third Millennium – somewhat out of kilter with what has just been explored – another type of pentecostal-charismatic church emerged in urban Africa. A perceptive African Christian scholar, the Revd Dr Kehinde Olabimtan, has described it thus: "In its external form it is sold out to western value system of clothing, music, wealth and urbanism. Although it draws much of these from the United States of America it is trans-national in spirit and vision and, at bottom, denigrates Africa's indigenous religions which are considered as having no value for advancing the cause of the Gospel in Africa. As a matter of fact, indigenous religions and cultural practices are seen as spiritual and social draw backs whose vestiges incapacitate their victims even when they have become Christians. They are therefore undesirable and are to be remedied by the process of spiritual deliverance through prayers" [6]. No sensitive Christian or serious scholar would denigrate traditional beliefs. Yet it is appropriate to recognise that Prophet Harris, for one, would undoubtedly have agreed with the understanding of the need for total renunciation of the old religion in order wholeheartedly to accept the Way of Jesus.

Wider Applications of this West African Study

The growth in the number of Christians in sub-Saharan West Africa from the mid-19th Century onwards was truly astounding. It reflected similar growth in the East and South of the continent. Then, not surprisingly, this massive growth was also matched by increased missionary zeal within African Churches of all types. For example, by the end of the 20th Century, much 'South-to-South' evangelism was happening across the countries of sub-Saharan Africa. Also, Africans became an important element in the 're-evangelisation of Europe'. For example many a central London church was sustained (or even increased in size) by an influx of African immigrants; and some wholly new, large African-led churches were established across Europe.

Yet within West Africa, the northward thrust of Christian faith was obstinately thwarted in the sahel by determined Muslim rulers, often from the Fulani ethnic group. It must be repeated that the religious 'dividing line' was not produced by geography – in the form of the Sahara Desert - but by spiritual, political and social pressures. From the early 19th Century onwards, the 10th degree of latitude had represented an apparently insurmountable 'religious fault-line'. Tragic events on a global scale in the first decade of the 21st Century accentuated this dividing line in West Africa but they did not create it. Failure to recognise this crucial historical perspective has compounded the challenge to Christian mission in Muslim lands.

Judgements about the impact of Christian faith as brought to West Africa by European missionaries are particularly susceptible both to over-generalization and to the inevitable bias of whoever wrote them. Therefore, let Dr Olabimtan, as a well-accredited contemporary African historian, have the final comment on the subject: "The history of the church in Africa is a long one whose roots are deep in antiquity. Critics, both in the Western world and on the continent of Africa, have often insinuated that Christianity is a white man's religion used to soften Africans before their final subjugation in the colonial era. This assertion is highly prejudiced and does not take into account the dynamics that gave birth to missions and the altruistic motives that made men and women lay down their lives in droves for the spiritual and social regeneration of Africa. This is not to argue that all missionaries did well. It only means that each situation of missionary encounter with African society must be evaluated in its context; that is within the realities that shaped and informed the encounter. And when that is done, in spite of all the minuses that accompanied missions, it will be seen that, at bottom, Christian missions elevated Africa" [7].

NOTES AND REFERENCES

"Ethiopia shall soon stretch out her hands unto God" in the chapter title sub-heading is a translation of Psalm 68: 31, AV.

1   MacCulloch, op.cit., p.880
2   McCall, Malcolm, <u>Kailondo's Luawa and British Rule</u>, unpublished D.Phil. thesis, University of York, 1974, p.518
3   Oral testimony from the Revd Gilbert Hall in direct conversation with the author, in the early years of the 21st Century. The catechist was the father of the Revd Michael Stevens. Towards the end of the 20th. Century the Revd Stevens was Secretary of the Methodist Conference in Nigeria. When the author recounted the story of this catechist in a Methodist ministerial meeting in Nigeria in 2009, without disclosing the catechist's name, the Revd Stevens, without any prompting, leaned over to his neighbor and said, "He's speaking about my father".
4   MacCulloch, op.cit., p886
5   Ibid., p. 964. Note the seminal phrase "her own hands".
6   Cliff College International Training Centre, Lecture Notes by the Revd Dr Kehinde Olabimtan, <u>African Church History</u>, 2011
7   Ibid.

AFRICAN PERSPECTIVES: SOME DISCUSSION POINTS

1   Considering the history of West Africa since the mid-19th Century, how would <u>you</u> explain the astounding expansion of Christian faith? Relate your response to your own specific local area.

2   Prophet Harris tolerated polygamy, but preached strongly against the sin of adultery. In the context of African culture, and in the light of biblical teaching, was he right?

3   Outline the growth of Christian faith in your local area. Try to identify the driving factors behind this growth? Were there any negative elements which tended to limit growth? How were ordinary villagers impacted by this newly-introduced Christian faith? How was society in general, and its traditional institutions, affected?

CHAPTER EIGHT

THE 20TH CENTURY GLOBAL PENTECOST

"The promise of the Holy Spirit"

Origins of the modern Pentecostal Movement

Sometimes, 20th Century Pentecostalism has been portrayed as a totally new and unexpected movement, suddenly and volcanically erupting, largely from within Protestantism, during that century. This is a distortion. The modern 'Pentecostal movement' can in fact be traced back through the previous centuries for at least two hundred years, and contains elements from a wide variety of sources. For example, the numerically small Moravian church was a key contributor in the development of emphasis on the work of the Holy Spirit.

The Moravians were crucial in the 18th Century in pioneering the European-based Protestant missionary movement. As has been demonstrated earlier in this book, they also deeply influenced John Wesley's search for saving faith. Basically, 'baptism in the Holy Spirit' is implicit in Moravian Church history; and explicitly, in 1727, the experience of a powerful work of the Holy Spirit in their Herrnhut Christian community resulted in their amazingly fruitful, prayer-centred, missionary-envisioned ministry. Similarly, John Wesley's designated successor, the Revd John Fletcher, popularized a view of sanctification as being received by means of a 'baptism with the Holy Spirit'. Reformed Christians, heirs of Jonathan Edwards, (who ministered in the American colonies) were likewise impressed by this scriptural idea of 'baptism in the Holy Spirit'. Some proponents of this doctrine used the term 'Second Blessing' to describe it. Yet generally Reformed theologians were wary of suggestions in Wesley's holiness teaching, that 'being filled with the Holy Spirit' was linked with the possibility of instant perfection as a gift. But in the later part of the 19th Century, various groups such as the Keswick Holiness Movement in Britain, took up some of these themes.

A defining moment in the story of 20th Century Pentecostalism came in Azusa Street in Los Angeles in 1906. There, a mixed-race congregation, with opportunities for both black and female leadership, was meeting in a rented former African Methodist Church building. The leader at Azusa Street was William Joseph Seymour, an African-American. He was preaching that God would "send a new Pentecost", if only people prayed for one. In mid-1906, the congregation had a sudden communal experience of the gift of tongues. Thereafter revival broke out in this 'Apostolic Faith Mission' in Azusa Street, such that for over three years, they held three services a day, seven days a week. The worship and preaching combined elements from the white American holiness movement with the exuberant worship-style typical of ex-slaves from the American South. (Though note, in the Afro-American exuberance, much angst of spirit, and a deep yearning for real freedom – echoed in songs such as "Steal away to Jesus … I ain't got long to stay here.") The expressive worship and praise at Azusa Street included shouting and dancing. The admixture of tongues and other charisms with black music and worship styles created a new and indigenous form of pentecostalism that was to prove extremely attractive to disinherited and deprived people, both in North America and other continents of the world. In particular, the mixing of races at Azusa Street provided one of the most striking external impressions that 'a new thing' was taking place, for this happened against the backdrop of the segregation and racism prevalent at that time in the Southern USA. A white Azusa Street member movingly noted, 'The color line was washed away in the blood'.

During the 20th Century, in Latin America, sub-Saharan Africa and Asia, Pentecostalism became a major expression – perhaps the major expression – of Christian faith. But how did this happen? The accepted narrative of this sudden and amazing worldwide growth of Pentecostalism is that news from Azusa Street spread quickly around the world because of new methods of communication recently invented: the telegraph and the telephone. Moreover, the establishment of regular, comparatively-speedy trans-Atlantic liners meant that those in Europe, who were seriously gripped by the news from Azusa Street, could actually go and visit Los Angeles for themselves. However, references in the preceding two chapters of this book to Prophet Sokari Braide (Chapter 6) and Prophet Wade Harris (Chapter 7) challenge that accepted narrative. To reiterate: Braide's ministry was focused in the Niger Delta in the early years of the 20th Century and has been estimated to have reached over one million people. Harris' ministry began about a year later than that of Braide. The impact of Prophet Harris' mission was felt in several of the nations and ethnic groups surrounding his Liberian homeland; it was estimated that in the Côte d'Ivoire alone, between 1913 and 1915, at least one hundred thousand 'ordinary people' were converted through Harris' prophetic mission. However, the two ministries of Braide and Harris had no mutual contact until 1917: Braide and Harris had pursued similar prophetic ministries without any direct contact.

Both these prophetic movements led respectively by Braide and Harris may be understood as part of the exponential growth of Pentecostalism in the early 20th Century. Yet we have seen that both Braide and Harris' ministries were independent of each other. Moreover, they were both completely independent of events in Los Angeles. There is no evidence that either Braide or Harris was ever influenced by the Azusa Street revival during their entire ministries. Rather, both Braide and Harris were exercising a separate African Christian initiative moulded to African spiritual needs, neither of which depended on external influences. These crucial pieces of evidence may demand a fundamental revision of our understanding about how Pentecostal Christianity swept around the globe during the last century. From an African perspective, we are left to ponder on the work of a Sovereign God and His Holy Spirit, who cannot be controlled or steered by human agencies!

A new understanding of the meaning of 'Pentecostalism'

During much of the succeeding years of the 20th Century, 'Pentecostalism' (as it was generally described) grew exponentially in numbers world-wide. However, the sense of a global 'pentecostal community" – both geographically across the continents and also between various Christian groupings and churches – was somewhat clouded (perhaps even distorted?) by those whose very self-description was 'pentecostal'. This occurred because these 'Pentecostals' generally defined their distinctive characteristic as the use of *glossolalia,* the gift of 'tongues'; and 'speaking in tongues' was accepted as the crucial descriptor of pentecostal practice. However, it may be argued that 'the gift of tongues' should not be used as the sole descriptor of pentecostal practice, because it was not so used in the New Testament itself. Rather, typical outward manifestations of 'pentecostal' life and faith – fully endorsed in the New Testament – are better encapsulated in such phrases as 'signs and wonders;' 'miracles and healings;' 'prophecy'. Paul's First Letter to the Corinthian Christians, for example, particularly commends the gift of prophecy: "eagerly desire spiritual gifts, especially the gift of prophecy" (1 Cor. 14: 1, NIV), whilst adding words of caution concerning the exercise of the gift of tongues in the rest of the same chapter.

Furthermore, it can scarcely be doubted from Jesus' own words that the primary purpose of pentecostal "power from on high" was to produce effective preaching of the Good News " to all nations" (Luke 24: 47 and 49, NIV). In His own recorded words, therefore, Jesus did not focus on the gift of tongues as the primary evidence of this power from on high. Not surprisingly, then, the key observable evidence of the powerful impact of the Day of Pentecost, recorded in Acts Chapter 2, was 3,000 people coming to believe in Jesus on that day. In succeeding weeks and years many others were added to their number in what might be summarized as 'staggeringly effective evangelism'. If we understand the 'Pentecostal explosion' of the 20th Century in these terms, our perspective on Protestant Church History in that century may be considerably altered. To refer once more to Braide and Harris, applying to them this new perspective of 'effective evangelism' being the first evidence of the Holy Spirit's anointing, the impact of their ministries is most naturally to be understood as part of the 'Pentecostal explosion' of the 20th Century.

In Harris' case, there is also a unique extra dimension to consider when assessing the results of his preaching. He prophetically assured his converts that fuller Bible-based instruction would lead them on to a fuller discipleship of Jesus. "Wait and pray," he told his people. "Build churches, and one day missionaries will come to teach you the Way." Amazingly, his people waited faithfully for ten years for that prophecy to be fulfilled; but eventually as Methodist missionaries reached them in 1923, Harris' prophecy was fulfilled. Nearly 50,000 people were made members of the Methodist Church. From the perspective of Jesus' own promise about "power from on high," on the Day of Pentecost, Harris' Spirit-empowered ministry must surely be understood as a part of the 20th Century global 'Pentecostal explosion'. And understood from this perspective, a white British Methodist missionary's account of his first contact with Harris' converts – who had been patiently waiting for ten years for this moment – takes on an even greater significance. That missionary's name was was the Revd William Platt, and an extensive quotation is appropriate:

"There were hundreds of people in the streets awaiting me, for I happened to be the first missionary. I was taken into a long, low building and found six hundred people seated on the floor. On one wall was a picture of Elijah on Mount Carmel, praying fire from Heaven on his sacrifice while the prophets of Baal looked on. On another wall, John the Baptist was seen baptizing in Jordan. These pictures are symbolic of the religion of those people standing for repentance and righteousness, but not yet fully Christian.

'Harris baptized me ten years ago,' the leader of that meeting announced to the crowd. 'He told me to preach to the people, and so I have done. Now, Sir,' he went on, turning to me, we hand over ourselves and six other village congregations to your Church – two thousand of us in all – if you will only send us a teacher' "[1].

Surely such a narrative should be understood as a story which reflects, in one local situation, an example of the global 'Pentecostal explosion' in the 20th Century. This story becomes a 'pentecostal narrative' especially if the 'Day of Pentecost' is seen through the lens of Jesus' final promise to His followers in Luke 24: 49 to wait for power from on high in order to preach repentance to all nations. So the heart of Pentecost was described in terms of powerfully effective evangelism. Furthermore, William Platt's narrative provides further evidence of a hitherto largely unrecognised element in that 'explosion:' it consisted, globally, of many independent lines unconnected with each other, yet woven together by an unexpected continuity at a later point.

The Explosive Global Growth of Pentecostal Christianity

To many, as the new Pentecostalism began to cross continents, the wondrous thing was the way in which the Holy Spirit clearly moved inter-racially. Moreover, often those most powerfully touched were the poor and dispossessed, people who had suffered colonial or other kinds of political oppression. Commonly, they lacked formal education, and were without any worldly status. Out of great suffering, these were often the ones whom the Spirit of Jesus raised up (see 1Corinthians 1: 26 – 29). Some became known globally as respected leaders.

In terms of numbers, the story of Pentecostal growth cannot be precise: many Pentecostal churches – such as the African Independent Churches – do not set great store on counting numbers. Also, Pentecostal groupings are to be found within existing mainline churches, and numbers may not be easy to extract. However, Philip Jenkins, in careful research, suggests that by the beginning of the 21st Century, adherents of Pentecostal Christianity numbered hundreds of millions. He notes how historians of the 20th Century had devoted much time and space to political movements such as fascism and communism, which have largely failed. He continues, 'Since there were only a handful of Pentecostals in 1900, and several hundred million today, is it not reasonable to identify this as perhaps the most successful social movement of the past century?' [2]

The newer Pentecostal churches, together with charismatic groupings within traditional churches, tend to preach a deep personal faith, a communal orthodoxy in accordance with scriptural guidelines, and a mysticism of spirit together with the practice of puritanism. They take the Bible very seriously as the Word of God, and generally resist reinterpretation of the Scriptures as an attempt at adapting to 'the modern world' or 'changed social norms'. They preach messages which, to some, may appear simplistically charismatic, visionary, and apocalyptic. Prophecy is an everyday reality – and is taken seriously and acted on. Faith healing and exorcism are fundamental elements in normal Christian living. Detailed material needs are often the subject for earnest prayer. Much of this understanding of Biblical faith runs at odds with the numerically declining liberal Protestantism of some Western churches and of scholars in Europe and America.

Pentecostals and Charismatics in the later 20th Century

In the USA and in Western Europe, during the later decades of the 20th Century, members of 'mainline churches' began to experience for themselves 'a new Pentecost' and began to use charismatic gifts. But many of them did not leave their own denominational organizations. Rather, they tried to fit their new experience into the teaching and practice of their own churches. Such Christians, often networked in groupings within their own churches or trans-denominationally. They were generally known as 'charismatics' rather than 'Pentecostals'. The Catholic Church, as well as Protestant denominations, was affected by such groupings. In the last decades of the 20th Century, there were some signs that traditional churches were changing and adapting to this new spirituality. Indeed, as early as the Second Vatican Council, the Catholic Church affirmed, 'We need a new Pentecost'.

The definitive handbook <u>Operation World</u> affirms that in 2010 there were over 177 million pentecostals. If charismatics within non-charismatic denominations, together with charismatics in post-denominational networks, are added to members of historical pentecostal denominations, the numerical result is even more astounding: charismatics had multiplied from less than one million in 1900 to around 425 million in 2010. In other words, one decade into the new millennium, on the global Christian scene, there were nearly half a billion charismatics[3]. According to current projections, the global joint number of Pentecostal and charismatic believers should cross the one billion mark before 2050. "In terms of the global religions, there will be by that point roughly as many Pentecostals as Hindus, and twice as many as there are Buddhists"[4].

In the UK, the New Frontiers family of churches, (led by Terry Virgo) was able, amazingly, to combine Reformed theology with charismatic practice, focussing on global mission. In the USA, John Wimber and his Association of Vineyard Churches, began to teach that the gift of tongues was just one of many spiritual gifts described in the New Testament; so 'glossolalia' should not be regarded as the primary evidence of being 'baptized in the Spirit'. This change in emphasis helped some non-charismatic evangelicals to understand more sympathetically the whole 'charismatic movement' as it swept through many mainline churches.

However, the issue of 'signs and wonders and miracles' continued to be contentious for many Western evangelicals, tending to produce tensions between Western evangelicals who were charismatics, and those who were not. Significantly though, from a global perspective, the more fundamental division was more between the 'global South' and the European or American churches. For example, few Christians in the global South considered that there was any problem about preaching and praying for physical healing; but many Western Christians found themselves 'uncomfortable' when addressing these matters.

NOTES AND REFERENCES:

"The promise of the Holy Spirit" in the chapter sub-title is a quotation from Acts 2: 33, NRSV.

1   Platt, William J., <u>From Fetish to Faith: the Growth of the Church in West Africa</u>, (The Cargate Press, London, 1935) ps. 86-87

2   Jenkins, op. cit., ps. 8 – 9

3   Mandryk, Jason, <u>Operation World</u> (7th Edition, Biblica Publishing, Colorado Springs, USA, 2010) ISBN: 978 – 1 – 85078 – 861 – 4, ps. 3 – 4

4   Jenkins, p.9

5   Ibid. Jenkins provides a helpful summary of the social background, culture and life-style of a 'typical' global Pentecostal Christian. His summary has formed the basis of this section of the present chapter

AFRICAN PERSPECTIVES: SOME DISCUSSION POINTS

1   In seeking to understand the global explosion of Pentecostal Christianity, how would you comment on Jesus' own statement to the Jewish religious leader Nicodemus: "The wind blows where it chooses, and you hear the sound of it, but you do not know where it comes from or where it goes: so it is with everyone who is born of the Spirit" (John 3: 8, NRSV)?

2   Many charismatics would understand 'baptism in the Spirit' as integral to a full proclamation of the Gospel (e.g. the Full Gospel Businessmen's Association, a 20th Century para-church).This is also true of some denominational churches. For example, the International Church of the Foursquare Gospel would describe the Person of Jesus in the following way:

>   The Saviour
>   The Baptiser with the Holy Spirit
>   The Healer
>   The Soon-Coming King.

Such Christians would note that there are few specific promises concerning Jesus' ministry which are recorded in all four Gospels. Yet the statement, "He … will baptise with the Holy Spirit" (e.g. John 1: 33, NIV) is laid down as the crucial introduction to Jesus' ministry in all four. Especially in Luke-Acts, the key to the Apostles continuing the ministry of Jesus is this: "you will receive power when the Holy Spirit comes on you; and you will be My witnesses … to the ends of the earth" (Acts 1: 8, NIV). Therefore, it may be argued, Jesus Himself emphasizes that this empowering by the Holy Spirit is the 'hinge' on which swings the whole growth of the church and the coming of the Kingdom.

What is your response to this view?

CHAPTER NINE

"A NEW SONG . . . FROM THE ENDS OF THE EARTH" THE THIRD MILLENNIUM

At the beginning of the third millennium, the global Church was in a state of transition and even turmoil. A number of elements contributed to this time of radical change. However, one main underlying factor at work transforming the Church's life and mission at the turn of the Millennium was the distribution of Christianity's worldwide numerical strength and missionary vitality, both of which were increasingly focussed in the 'Majority South'. What is meant by the 'Majority South'? After WW2, during the years of the 'Cold War' between 'the West' and 'the East', the most populous regions of the globe became known as the 'Third World' or, later, the 'Developing World'. They are now often referred as the 'global South' or the 'majority South'. The term 'global South' was coined by the European Brandt Commission at the height of the Cold War, to denote those parts of the world outside North America, Europe and Japan. Of course, not all these other parts of the world are located in the southern hemisphere. The term 'South' is not so much about geographical location as about wealth and resources – or lack of them – in many of the countries referred to. 'Majority South' also emphasizes that this group includes all the most populous countries on earth – most of which continue to experience rapid population growth. Of course, there are discrepancies: Australia and New Zealand do not fit this description of the 'majority South'. Another common phrase for describing the 'Global South' is the

'Tri-continental World' – that is the world made up of South America, Africa and Asia.

Perhaps the most astounding development of the past hundred years has been the dramatic increase in numbers of self-confessed Christians in many 'majority South' countries. For example, in 1950, a list of the world's leading Christian countries would have included Britain, France, Spain and Italy, but the expectation is that none of these names would be represented in a corresponding list for 2050. In 1900 Europe was home to two-thirds of the world's Christian population; by 2010, the figure was less than a quarter. In the continent of Africa, in 1900 there were around 10 million Christians; by 2000 there were 360 million! So, Christianity's global 'centre of gravity' moved steadily southwards during the 20th Century to Africa, South America, South-East Asia and China. By 2005, Christians represented around 2.1 billion people, or about one-third of the world's population. There were some 531 million in Europe, with 226 million in North America: a total of 757 million people. But the majority lived in Africa (389 million), Latin America (511 million) and Asia (344 million): a total of 1,244 million. Projecting these figures into the future, by 2050 it is likely that only about one-fifth of the world's 3 billion Christians would be non-Hispanic whites! [1].

In fact, by the beginning of the 21st Century, the global 'centre of gravity' was already in the 'tri-continental world' of Africa, Asia and Latin America. This situation reflected not only the increasing number of Christians in these more southerly regions, but also the great dynamism of their Christian faith. These tri-continental Christians were generally Spirit-empowered, missionary-minded and expectant-hearted. Theirs was a faith seeming much closer to the 'Acts of the Apostles' model than the sort of Christian faith generally evident in Western Europe or the USA. 'If you want to see where it's all happening, go to Africa'; 'If you want to see Methodism as it is meant to be, go to Cuba'. Such anecdotal comments by West European Christian leaders are corroborated by much statistical evidence.

The statistics for Christian growth in Africa are particularly astounding. Christianity has grown to become the religion of almost half Africa's population, and nearly two-thirds of sub-Saharan Africa. From 1900 to 2010, Christian numbers grew from 9.1% of the population to 48.8%, and from 7.5 million to 504 million … Evangelical growth has been even more spectacular. In 1900 in Africa, evangelicals numbered 1.6 million (1.5%), but in 2010, there were 182 million (17.7% of the population). This is nearly as many as all evangelicals in the Americas combined and is the largest evangelical population of any continent. African evangelicals are also increasing at a faster rate than any other continent [2]. It is also significant that the annual rate of Christian growth (2.5% approx.) is higher than the population growth rate for the continent (2.3% approx.). The respected current-affairs magazine The Economist, with its most up-to-date-statistics in 2015, reported even more startling figures than those just quoted: 'According to the Centre for the Study of Global Christianity at Gordon-Conwell theological Seminary, in 1910 just 9% of the 100 million people on the African continent were Christian; today the share is 55% of a population of a billion … Sub-Saharan Africa is not only home to the world's most observant Christians; it is also the fastest-growing region on the planet by population.' No wonder The Economist headed the above article: 'The March of Christianity: The Future … is African' [3].

The typical life-style and theological outlook among 'Majority South' Christians are very different from that of ordinary European or American Christians. In material assets and 'disposable income' 'Majority South' Christians are likely to possess very little. They might not have access to an adequate water-supply for washing, irrigation of crops and provision for live-stock. Indeed, they might not have clean water even for drinking and cooking. Typically, adequate schools and medical facilities might also be lacking. Poverty, violence and poor governance are often endemic where they live. It was noteworthy that often the regions of the globe where Christian faith is advancing most noticeably are those areas where governments were most fragile, and therefore conflict most likely. Cultural norms are unlike those in 'Western Societies'. Moreover, the theological outlook of typical 'Majority South' Christians is based on different suppositions from their 'Western' counterparts.

A careful and respected African Church historian, Andrew Walls, has suggested the growing Christian faith in Africa represents not only a significant explosion in numbers, but also a distinctive new tradition of Christianity, comparable to that of Catholicism, Protestantism or Orthodoxy. This new 'African Christianity' is, Walls suggests, 'the standard Christianity of the present age, a demonstration model of its character'. It therefore follows that 'anyone who wishes to undertake serious study of Christianity these days needs to know something about Africa'[4]. Concentrating further on the 'African model' as it has developed over the last hundred years in Africa, three marked trends may be distinguished. First, dramatic numerical progress has been made by those 'mainline' Western-based churches that have remained conservative and traditional in their theology and practice: for example, the Anglicans in Nigeria. A second mark of the African model is the astonishing growth of Pentecostal churches in the 20th Century. A third mark is the huge increase in 'African Indigenous Churches'. These are new, non-traditional denominations which often seriously seek to accommodate Christian belief within their local tradition and culture. They are sometimes known as 'African Independent Churches'.

By most accounts, Pentecostal and Independent churches have hundreds of millions of members and adherents worldwide. Within a few decades, such denominations spread throughout all the continents, will conceivably represent the majority of all global Christians. Jenkins typifies their theology and practice: 'These new churches preach deep personal faith and communal orthodoxy, mysticism and puritanism, all founded on clear scriptural authority. They preach messages that, to a Westerner, appear simplistically charismatic, visionary, and apocalyptic. In this thought-world, prophecy is an everyday reality, while faith-healing, exorcism, and dream-visions are all fundamental parts of religious sensibility'[5]. 'Signs and wonders and miracles' are a natural part of the daily lives of such Christians, which is not surprising, considering that they feature so largely in Scripture. In the Old Testament, for example, great wonders are done by God in Egypt, to set His people free. In Acts, the LORD confirms the message through signs and wonders performed by the Apostles. This accords with the 'longer ending' of Mark's Gospel where Jesus commands: "'Go into all the world and preach the Good News to everyone, everywhere' . . . . And the disciples went everywhere and preached, and the Lord worked with them, confirming what they said by many miraculous signs" (Mark 16: 15 and 20, NIV). Other key features of normal spiritual life among most 'Majority South' Christians are expectations of material prosperity and physical healing. This is not surprising, when many live in grinding poverty, in areas endemically affected by life-threatening illnesses.

Forces for Radical Change within the Worldwide Church

In examining the global character of Christian faith at the beginning of the Third Millennium, several other forces for radical change may be identified, in addition to the Faith's 'centre of gravity' moving to the Global South. Firstly, and for many Westerners, unexpectedly 'religion' became an increasingly powerful geopolitical force. In fact, many people (especially in politically volatile and fragile regions of the world) began to place religious affiliation as the major defining characteristic of their identity. Often, for them, religion came before nationality, ethnicity or (even) language.

On 11th September 2001, Islamist terrorists attacked and demolished the 'Twin Towers,' landmark buildings in central New York, involving the deaths of hundreds of people working in those buildings at that time. Usually referred to as '9/11', this tragic event was a defining moment in many ways: not least because it demonstrated how religious faith was still a major global motivator – some would say <u>the</u> major motivator – in the lives of many, and could not be ignored or sidelined in the way that sceptical Western academics and media outlets had tended to do in the last decades of the 20th Century. A recognition of this reality came surprisingly in a book from two editors of <u>The Economist</u>: this book was entitled <u>God is Back</u>. It notes that 'religion is playing a much more important role in public and intellectual life ... religion is part of the modern world.' [6] In the USA, for example, the growing strength and influence of Christian faith has been especially noticeable in the years since the Second World War. Billy Graham might be mentioned as one global Christian preacher who was active from the early 1950s onwards: it is claimed that he has spoken 'live' to more people than any other person in world history – and he spoke as a Christian Evangelist. His one driving concern has been so to present 'Christ crucified and risen' that people should make a decision to turn to Him in faith. He would always invite people at the end of his meetings to leave their seats and walk forward to the front as a sign of making a decision for Christ. Over the years 'at least 3.2 million people walked to the Cross to receive Jesus Christ as their Saviour' [7].

A second force for radical change was that the world Church like other international institutions, was impacted by the process known as 'globalization'. This is a 'shorthand title' for a process which has increasingly affected all peoples and nations of the world in the last decades of the 20th Century. It has been memorably encapsulated in one sentence: 'The world is now a global village'. This process has affected economics, politics and society; therefore, it has naturally impacted the Church as well. For example, in relation to international Christian mission, travel has become much quicker, easier and cheaper. In the 17th Century, it took maybe a year to sail to China, but in the 21st Century, it may only take 20 hours to fly there! Moreover – and perhaps crucially - mobile phones and internet access have deeply changed not only the communications, but also the perceptions of peoples on a global scale. Many of the world's people, even many of the economically poorest, have immediate access to almost unlimited amounts of information, together with huge varieties of opinion and the interpretation of it. One result of all this is that many more people know of the difficulties, persecutions, and triumphs of local and national Christian communities around the planet.

However, there has also been a strong reaction to the perceived 'homogenizing' and 'standardizing' brought about by globalization. There has been a growth of a populist nationalism, politically, culturally and ethnically emphasizing the distinctive characteristics of different groups. Ethnic minorities have demanded independence from larger nations. The last decades of the 20th century saw the break-up of Yugoslavia; genocide in Rwanda and Burundi; separatist movements in many countries. For example, serious threats were posed in Spain (by the Basques and

Catalonians) and Indonesia (in the Aceh region). Within the United Kingdom, despite a number of powers being devolved to a Scottish Parliament in the 1990s, the idea of Scotland becoming completely independent (from England) retained a considerable appeal for many Scots. These 'nationalist' movements were inevitably reflected within the churches – sometimes by majority South Church leaders displaying a sturdy independence from other, often ex-colonial, 'international' denominational churches. Positively, the universal Church often made a powerful contribution in this global ferment stirred up by globalisation. New Testament teaching is that we are 'the one body of Christ worldwide, while still enjoying the local church with its more intimate identity and fellowship' [8].

A third increasing pressure on the 21st Century Church was that 'the blood of the martyrs' is still 'the seed of the Church'. Persecution of Christians and violence towards them has increased in recent decades – and continues to do so. Surprisingly, it has been estimated that there were more Christian martyrs in the 20th Century than in all the previous 'Christian' centuries added together; and it seems that this terrible trend is continuing into the 21st Century. Korea provides one such example, between the late 19th Century and the late 20th Century, of the many deaths and martyrdoms among Christian pioneers, which at length led to amazing church growth. Many in the 19th Century assumed that Korean culture was so impervious to foreigners and so isolationist in attitude that there was no Gospel opportunity in that region. When a Welsh missionary, Robert Thomas, landed in Korea with Bibles to distribute among Chinese-speaking people, he was attacked and died even as he stumbled ashore, pressing his precious Bibles into the hands of his murderers. But in 1906, forty years later, in a New Year Bible Study when about 1500 people had gathered in the same area where Thomas was killed, the Holy Spirit swept through the meeting in revival power. By the beginning of the 21st Century, South Korea was the country which had sent out the second-largest number of Christian missionaries of any country on the planet (second only to the USA), and is arguably one of the most 'christianized' nations on earth. However, the government in North Korea so far remains one of those most violently opposed to Christian faith [9].

It is increasingly agreed that, in the last few decades, the growth of Christianity in China represents the greatest large-scale Christian conversion movement the world has ever seen. In the book <u>God is Back</u>, this movement is described as 'what may well be the biggest advance of Christianity ever. The Chinese government's own figures show the number of Christians rising from fourteen million in 1997 to twenty-one million in 2006, with an estimated fifty-five thousand official Protestant churches and forty-six hundred Catholic churches . . . . . but these figures exclude both underground house churches and the underground Catholic Church, which is bigger than the official one. A conservative guess is that there were at least sixty-five million Protestants in China and twelve million Catholics – more believers than members of the Communist Party! Some local Christians think the flock is well over one hundred million [10]. Even that may be an underestimate! Yet at what cost in terms of suffering by Christian pastors and ordinary church members this has come about. The persecution of Christians during the "Cultural Revolution" years of 1966 to 1976 is sometimes too searing to contemplate: for instance the account by Brother Yun in <u>The Heavenly Man</u> [11,] Christians were imprisoned, beaten, tortured and killed. Bibles were burnt. Some Christians were nailed alive to the walls of their church buildings. But the greater the persecution, the more people followed Christ.

In describing the forces for radical change affecting global Christianity at the beginning of the Third Millennium, a third developing trend is significant: global mission and evangelism were increasingly 'South-to-South' and 'South-to-North'. By the end of the 20th Century, vibrant churches in countries like South Korea and Nigeria had started sending missionaries to other 'majority South' regions. Sometimes there were specific reasons for this development. For example, developments in the Middle East in the early years of the 21st Century seemed to present the possibility of new opportunities for sensitive Christian mission in some situations. Not for white Europeans or Americans, however, but for a Christian from the 'Majority South' who might just find a Gospel opportunity.

There were also thoughts of the 're-evangelization' of Europe by missionaries from the 'Global South'. Partly as a result of migration, many 'Majority South' Christians found themselves in a missionary situation in cities in Western Europe. For example, attendance at Sunday Christian Services in central London grew at the turn of the Millennium as a result of immigration from (often Pentecostal) sub-Saharan Africa and from (mainly Catholic) Eastern Europe. The largest church in the United Kingdom in the last years of the 20th Century – Kingsway International Christian Centre in London – was led by Nigerians headed by Pastor Awolowo. Indeed, it was numerically the largest local church established in Britain for almost 200 years! In 2015, it was recognised that the fastest-growing Church-grouping within Britain was the Redeemed Christian Church. This grouping started in Nigeria, but is now established in more than 100 countries, with more than 750 local churches in the UK alone. Out of an estimated half-a-million Pentecostal Christians, perhaps a quarter belong to the Redeemed Church [12]. So, in an unexpected development, those European countries which, in the previous three centuries, had been the <u>senders</u> of missionaries to the rest of the world, started to become the <u>receivers</u> of missionaries from the 'majority South'. Pastor Agu Irukwu, head of the Redeemed Church's executive council in the UK, has poignantly described it thus: 'British missionaries abandoned everything to come to Africa, and many did not return. So, I feel a great debt to Great Britain for the people who made the sacrifices to bring the Gospel to Africa. A lot of us were educated at good missionary schools. I feel that I am here to pay this debt back because the UK has become so secular' [13].

Some of these radical changes, transforming the worldwide church's life and mission at the turn of the Millennium, were so new and revolutionary that they seemed to be creating a serious crisis. Others were part of a steady process, moving so quietly as to be barely distinguishable in the short term – but still part of the same deep and inexorable process of change. Taken together, these elements of transformation were perhaps as great and as significant as any which had affected the Church over the preceding five hundred years.

During much of the 20th Century, many Western intellectuals and academics cynically assumed that religious belief had ceased to be anything but the private 'hobby' of an increasingly small global minority of people, and of only marginal significance in public affairs at the national or international level. How wrong this presumption proved to be. By the end of the first decade of the new Millennium, the authors of <u>God is Back</u> were able to affirm: 'the secularization theorists are wrong to claim that modernity and religion are incompatible. Religion has always thrived in the world's most modern country ... Now it is also thriving in much of the modernizing world too, from Asia to the Middle East ... It is moving back toward the center of intellectual life'. [14] 'If you want to understand the politics of this century', declares the book's cover, 'you cannot afford to ignore God, whether you believe in Him or not'.

NOTES AND REFERENCES

"A new song <u>from</u> the ends of the earth" in the chapter title is from Isaiah 42: 10 (NIV), and contrasts with the Scripture reference in the title of Chapter Six: "<u>to</u> all nations". (Underlining added.)

1   Jenkins, P., <u>The Next Christendom</u> (revised and expanded, OUP, New York, 2007) ISBN: 978 – 0 – 19 – 518307 – 8, ps.2-3

2   Mandryk, Jason, <u>Operation World</u> (, Biblica Publishing, Colorado Springs, CO 80921, USA, revised 7ᵗʰ Edition 2010) ISBN: 978 – 1 – 85078 – 861 – 4) p.33

3   "The March of Christianity: The future of the world's most popular religion is African," in <u>The Economist</u>, 25 December 2015

4   Jenkins, op. cit., p.4, quoting a statement by Professor Andrew Walls

5   ibid., p.8.

6   Micklethwait, J. and Woolridge, A., <u>God is Back</u> (Allen Lane, Penguin Books, London, 2009) ISBN: 978 – 0 – 713 - 99902 – 0, p. 27

7   'Obituary, Billy Graham' in The <u>Economist</u>, 3 March 2018, p.86

8   Goldsmith, M., <u>Get a Grip on Mission</u> (IVF, Nottingham, UK, 2006) ISBN: 978 – 1 – 84474 – 126 – 7, p. 39

9   A popularly-told narrative of the incredible growth of Christian faith in the southern Korea is to be found in Whittaker, C., <u>Great Revivals</u> (Kingsway, Eastbourne, revised 2005) ISBN: 1 – 84291 – 222 – 4

10 Micklethwait and Woolridge, op. cit., ps 4 - 5

11 Brother Yun, <u>The Heavenly Man</u> (Monarch Books, London, 2002) ISBN: 1 – 85424 – 597 – X

12 These statistics come from information provided on the British BBC One TV programme, "Songs of Praise", broadcast on Sunday 24 May 2015 (Pentecost Sunday).

13 Quoted in an article by Damian Arnold in <u>The Times</u> newspaper, Saturday 21 November 2015

14 Micklethwait and Woolridge, op. cit., ps. 354 - 355

AFRICAN PERSPECTIVES: DISCUSSION POINT

Some observers delineate Modern Church History in the following way:

16th and 17th Centuries: the era of 'justification by faith';

17th and 18th Centuries: the era of 'making disciples of all nations';

20th and 21st Centuries: the era of 'the outpouring of the Spirit'.

What is your understanding? What signs have there been in your own geographical area of "the outpouring of the Spirit"? Has your area been impacted spiritually?

CONCLUSION

This study was undertaken in order to look from an African perspective at the Reformation Movement which began in Europe. Its primary aim was to offer a better means of entry into Reformation history for African students. However, seeing things from an African viewpoint has, unexpectedly, provided, for the present writer, new understandings of the global 'on-going Reformation' up to the present day. This has happened partly because ongoing reformation movements, in the last hundred years, have especially affected sub-Saharan Africa (together with South America, South East Asia and China), as compared with Europe.

In examining Modern Church History, the present writer has, on the one hand, rejected the historiographical method which aims to study the past in the light of the present; to this writer – as to most historians – it would represent a distorted and distorting understanding of historiography. So the intention has been to avoid allowing recent African Christian history to dictate the description and analysis of Modern Church History generally. On the other hand, however, it must be conceded that historical studies cannot be completely detached from the historian's own contemporary milieu and faith-commitment. Indeed, personally, it has been a transforming experience to rewrite, from an African perspective, some aspects of world-wide Modern Church History, having lived in Africa surrounded by and immersed in dynamic and ongoing Christian 'reformations and revivals.' This has proved a very different experience from writing within a European context, where such things are now, largely, distant memories.

The Scriptures themselves often describe transformational movements through the image of freely flowing streams of "living water" (Ezekiel 47). Indeed, Jesus' own words in John 4: 14 might be cited. This imagery – somewhat extended - may prove helpful in the context of Modern Church History. The 16th and 17th Centuries in Europe may be compared to a dam bursting, and its spiritual 'reservoir' – epitomised in the phrase "by grace, through faith" – flooding out across Europe. Before long, this 'living water' was flowing inter-continentally, so that by the mid-17th Century the New World was already being impacted. By the beginning of the 19th Century, a European missionary movement was touching Africa and Asia as well; and by the end of that century, Christian faith – in both Protestant and Catholic manifestations – had been widely established throughout the globe. Thus, the 18th and 19th Centuries may be characterised as 200 years of global Christian mission. A hundred years later, by the end of the 20th Century, although faith in Jesus as the Christ had ebbed in Europe, the 'global flow' of that faith had grown almost unimaginably in both extent and numbers throughout most of the other inhabited continents. Therefore, the 20th and 21st Centuries may be viewed as the era of a global outpouring of the Holy Spirit "on all flesh" (Joel 2: 28). Such an outline may be contested as romantically inaccurate, unacceptably simplistic or academically naïve, but it seems to correlate with the experience of many African people. Moreover, it highlights one crucial element in Modern Church History which has often been neglected: the worldwide, ongoing, exponential global growth of 'reformation' and revival-related movements. And five hundred years after Wittenburg, there is no sign of decline in their power and impact in any continent other than Europe.

However, the main thrust of these studies – surveying the Protestant Reformation from an African perspective – has not been to demonstrate global numerical growth. This has already been well documented by a variety of writers, even though their findings may not yet have been fully digested by church historians. Rather, this present writer's discovery – surprising to himself – has been the unexpected threads of continuity which may be discerned in the global spread of the Protestant Christian faith, especially in relation to the African continent. These 'threads of continuity' may be seen across continents and through centuries. The continuity is perceived essentially in this: from the first decades of the Reformation through to the first decades of the 21st Century, there is a consistent element of what – in shorthand – might be called 'pentecostal theology and practice.' This is a continuity which has been largely ignored, 'down-played, or dismissed by many church historians. But those who have read thus far will have discovered that this unexpected continuity has become pivotal to the present book's *raison d'être*.

To summarise this continuity, it may first be noted that within a few decades of Wittenberg, George Wishart was exercising his ministry in Scotland. The Scottish Reformation demonstrated all the scriptural features generally included in the term 'pentecostal' (though not, of course, using the particular 20th Century connotation of that word). A continuity may then be discerned in the following centuries of Scottish Church History, clearly observable, for example, in the lives and ministries of the 17th Century South-West Scottish Covenanters (Chapter Four).

Moreover, the Spirit-anointed' weekend-long 'Holy Fairs' which were such a remarkable feature of Scottish Protestantism in the late 16th and early 17th Centuries were 'exported' to the American colonies in succeeding decades. There, they transmuted into 'Camp Meetings'. These Camp Meetings demonstrated that same power, emotion, and spiritual transformation often associated with remarkable 'movements of the Holy Spirit' throughout the centuries of Modern Church History.

From this perspective, similar continuities begin to appear elsewhere; for example, the early 18th Century outpouring of the Holy Spirit on the Herrnhut Moravian Community (Chapter Five). It surely links with the 'baptism in the Holy Spirit,' which Whitfield, the Wesley brothers, and others, experienced on 1 January 1739. This, in turn, resonates with the 'second blessing' teaching of such leaders as Fletcher of Madeley (Wesley's designated successor). In turn, this 'second blessing' teaching fed into those 19th Century 'Holiness Movements' which are generally considered as significant contributors to the 20th Century global Pentecostal 'explosion.'

Out of this discussion, as viewed from the African continent, the burgeoning growth of Independent African Churches in the 20th and 21st Centuries may be perceived in a new light. Now, they may appear not only as demonstrations of a distinctly African response to the Gospel, but also as part of a thread of Protestantism which stretches back to the early 16th Century. This 'pentecostal thread,' also causes events such as the Azusa Street revival (Chapter 8) to look less unprecedented than they had previously appeared.

As we conclude, some readers may be frustrated that this book has seemed so limited in its scope. They may suggest that a better title for this book might have been: 'Selective aspects of Protestant Reformation History, seen mainly from a West African perspective.' This criticism has validity, as has already been briefly acknowledged in the Introduction to this volume. However, the 'developing reformation' portrayed in the second half of this book presents a complicated picture (especially with regard to the Protestant aspect) which resists simplistic stereotypes. So maybe the best that can be achieved, in a work examining the broad sweep of five hundred years of history, is simply to select as many specific examples as scope and space will allow in order to illustrate basic themes amid the developing complexity. (Maybe in more general terms, competent historiography consists of wise selectivity accompanied by sensitive interpretation.) Hudson-Taylor's China Inland Mission (Chapter 6) represents one indication of a growingly-complex picture, where new understandings of mission began to be practised. For example, it was 'non-denominational' in outlook, accepting all potential missionaries who could accept a simple, basic statement of Christian faith. Moreover, its headquarters was based in China, where the mission was focussed, not in Europe or America. For a second example of the growingly-complex picture, take the Pentecostals of the Twentieth Century, who, largely, did not attach the descriptor 'Protestant' to their movements, even though they <u>were</u> protestant in their central doctrines (Chapter 8). A final example of growing complexity might be the 'Charismatics' of the late 20th Century, who were largely uninterested in labels, and were generally ready to 'share fellowship' with like-minded believers across the whole spectrum of the Christian Churches, whether Orthodox, Roman Catholic, or Protestant (Chapter

9). Thus the starkness of such divisions as 'Protestant' and 'Catholic' have become blurred, and an attempt to maintain clear boundary lines round the word 'Protestant' might inhibit insightful analysis.

Much of the subject material in this present book will be familiar to any teacher or lecturer in Modern Church History. However, in maintaining an African perspective, three new understandings of specific events have gained increasing significance [1]. The first new understanding concerns Luther's statement about his new birth. Of course, Luther's words have been frequently quoted by his biographers. However, from a viewpoint within 21st Century Africa, 'new birth' is widely assumed and discussed in Christian circles: this stands in contrast to frequent reticence and doubts within mainline European Christian communities about personal testimony to 'conversion experience'. Moreover, it is generally and openly assumed in Africa that new birth is the necessary starting point for Christian pilgrimage. Therefore, the significance of Luther's own words (as he wrote about his personal spiritual struggles in the years before 1517) are highlighted in a new way, and better understood as the critical starting-point of the Reformation, inner transformation preceding outward demonstration.

Second, the experience of John Wesley on the night of 1st January 1739 assumed a new significance when seen from within the milieu of an 'outpouring of the Holy Spirit' which is affecting many areas of sub-Saharan. A clearer understanding may thereby be gained of the experience of Wesley and the others that night. The conclusion is that the event may best be described as 'Baptism in the Holy Spirit', and the subsequent beginnings of the Methodist movement are seen in a different light as a result.

Third, and finally, is a point crucial to this present book's focus, which might also provide a starting point for further studies. As was highlighted in Chapter Eight, recent historical research in West Africa suggests a new dimension concerning the 20th Century global pentecostal movement. This dimension surely needs taking into account in future historiography. As has been seen, Prophet Wade Harris and Prophet Sokari Braide were working contemporaneously in West Africa. They pursued parallel 'signs and wonders' ministries, with multiple thousands of people being deeply affected by each of them. Yet they never met, or had any contact with each other, until late on in their ministries, years after the movements which bore their names had taken distinctive shapes and touched the lives of masses of local African people. Likewise, and crucial to the understanding of the global 20th Century Pentecostal movement, they had no contact with, or knowledge of, what was happening in Azusa Street. The 'spiritual outpouring' each experienced was not only independent of each other. It was also independent of other global movements which were occurring in the same early years of the 20th Century - even before 'Azusa Street. Looking more widely, this was also happening in other areas of the globe. For example, the 'Welsh Revival' in Britain started in 1904, before Azusa Street. The 'Korean Revival' in Asia might also be cited.

How may this be explained? Most Western historians – writing from within a framework of Enlightenment rationalism – would reject any notion of divine intervention, finding it academically unacceptable. Yet from a framework of vibrant African Christian faith, nothing seems more natural than Dr. Ekebusi's conclusion: 'God in his sovereignty can cause a person to experience Pentecost without prior interaction with any Pentecostal group' [2]. Moreover, in addition to individual persons, whole Christian communities can evidently experience 'reformation revival' without prior contact with 'pentecostalism', and without specific teaching on the subject. From this perspective, Azusa Street does not so much represent an initial 'springboard' for a world-wide exponential pentecostal explosion, but rather one incidence of local Christian 'people movements' which were 'exploding' around the globe, mostly independent of each other, at roughly the same time.

Thus, the present writer diffidently suggests new approaches in some aspects of Modern Church History. Naturally, the themes and conclusions in this volume require more exploration by other historians in different geographical, historical and ecclesiastical settings. Yet in essence, this present book is offered, humbly, as a possible pointer towards a different sort of historiography, requiring the need for a new attitude on the part of the historian himself; because 'what you see and hear' depends not only on where you are standing; it also depends on 'what sort of person you are.'

NOTES AND REFERENCES

[1]   In relation to these 'three new understandings', an attempt has been made to refer to primary sources rather than secondary sources. These primary sources are referenced in the Notes and References at the end of each chapter.

[2]   Ekebusi, op. cit., ps. 231 – 232

SELECT BIBLIOGRAPHY OF RECENTLY PUBLISHED WORKS

Ekebusi, C, <u>The Life and Ministry of Prophet Garrick Sokari Braide: Elijah the Second of Niger Delta, Nigeria (c.1882 – 1918)</u>, (Peter Lang, Bern, Switzerland, 2015) ISBN: 978 – 3 – 0343 – 1878

The Revd Dr Ekebusi's careful research introduces a hitherto little-known African Christian leader, who exercised a powerful prophetic and evangelistic ministry, independent of the simultaneous outpouring of the Holy Spirit in other continents. As an Igbo Methodist Minister, Dr Ekebusi offers valuable insights and understandings concerning Prophet Braide as the prototype African Christian Prophet. He preceded many other African prophetic ministries in the 20th Century.

Goldsmith, M, <u>Get a grip on Mission</u> (IVP, Nottingham, UK, 2006) ISBN: 978 – 1 – 84474 – 126 – 7

A sympathetic and insightful personally-involved account of global Christian Mission in the early 21st Century, from a 'white European' with considerable personal experience of his subject.

Gonzalez, J.L., <u>The History of Christianity Vol. 2: The Reformation to the Present Day</u> (HarperCollins, NY, USA, revised and updated 2010) ISBN: 978 – 0 – 06 – 185589 – 4

Professor Gonzalez, originally from Cuba, has concentrated his academic career on developing programmes for the theological education of

Hispanics. This emphasis provides a freshness of approach and opens up new perspectives on his subject. It provides new insights for readers, whether they are themselves Hispanics or not. This volume has been a source of inspiration to the present writer in pursuing a distinctively African perspective.

Jenkins, P, <u>The Next Christendom</u> (OUP, New York, revised and expanded 2007) ISBN: 978 – 0 – 19 – 518307

An authoritative, and well-researched seminal work, which describes the shift in Christianity's global 'centre of gravity' from Europe and North America to the "Global South" during the later twentieth century.

Liarden, R., <u>God's Generals: The Revivalists</u> (Whittaker House, PA, USA, 2008) ISBN: 978 – 1 – 60374 – 095 – 1

A popularly written biographical account of some well-known names in this area from the 18th Century to the present-day. It is written with passion and enthusiasm, and provides insightful comment.

MacCulloch, D, A History of Christianity (Allen Lane, London, 2009) ISBN: 978 – 0 713 – 99869

Professor MacCulloch's widely acclaimed book interprets Christian history as a record of both human achievement and human frailty.

Mandryk, J, <u>Operation World</u> (Biblica Publishing, Colorado Springs, USA, 7th Edition 2010) ISBN 978 – 1 – 85078 – 861 – 4

An invaluable source of global data, documenting the numerical growth of Christianity.

Micklethwait, J and Woolridge, A, <u>God is Back</u> (Allen Lane, Penguin Books, London, 2009) ISBN: 978 – 0 – 713 – 99902

A remarkable book by senior editors of <u>The Economist</u> magazine (perhaps the most respected weekly analysis of global current affairs in the English-speaking world). The authors insist that, to understand politics in the 21st Century, 'you cannot afford to ignore God'.

Milburn, G., Primitive Methodism (Epworth Press, Peterborough, 2002) ISBN 0 – 7162 – 05548

A brief but seminal book, especially in its examination of the origins and early growth of Primitive Methodism.

Ryrie, A, Being Protestant in Reformation Britain (OUP, Oxford, 2013) ISBN: 978 – 0 – 19 – 956572

Professor Ryrie unearths, through much meticulous research, the way in which the Reformation impacted individuals and their groups, as seen through the writings of contemporaries. Anyone wanting to write ethnographic Christian history will learn a great deal from Professor Ryrie's method.

Ryrie, A, "George Wishart: Scotland's Turbulent Prophet" in George Wishart Quincentennial Conference Proceedings (ed. Dotterweich, M, www.wishart.org, 2014 ISBN: 978 – 1 – 326 – 0392 – 5)

Professor Ryrie helpfully underlines what others at the Quincentennial Conference also demonstrated: that Wishart represents the beginnings of a Reformed Protestant tradition which recognised the ongoing experience of prophecy, signs, wonders, miracles and healings.

Schmidt, LE, Holy Fairs: Scotland and the making of American revivalism (Eerdmans, Grand Rapids, Michigan, 2nd edition with new Preface 2001) ISBN: 0 – 8028 – 4966 – 0

Ground-breaking research, which shows how Reformation practice and theology were crossing continents (in this case from Europe to America) within a 100 years of the beginning of the Reformation.

Stanford, P. Martin Luther Catholic Dissident (Hodder and Stoughton, London, 2017) ISBN 978 – 1 – 473 – 62167

This work was published in time for the 500th anniversary of Martin Luther's posting of the 95 Wittenberg Theses. It draws on the Weimarer Ausgabe, a complete collection of all Luther's writings, published in 2009. A perceptive and sympathetic study, it seeks to enter into some of Luther's heart-rending struggles as he came to assured faith in Jesus. The present writer found it especially enlightening on 'Justification by faith', ps. 93 – 99.

Skevington Wood, A, The Burning Heart – John Wesley: Evangelist (Bethany Fellowship, Minneapolis, US, 1978) ISBN 0 – 87123 – 043 – 7

The Revd Dr Skevington Wood was a Methodist minister, and a church historian, who became Principal of the evangelical Methodist Lay Training Cliff College, Derbyshire, in England. Dr Wood provides an insightful and sympathetic account of Wesley's life and ministry, which the present writer has found most useful.

Whittaker, C, Great Revivals (Kingsway, Eastbourne, UK, revised 2005) ISBN: 1 – 978 – 84474 – 518307

A popularly written, sympathetic summary of worldwide revivals from the early 18th to the early 21st centuries.

Woodbridge, JD and James, FA, Church History Vol. 2: From Pre-Reformation to the Present Day (Zondervan, Michigan, 2013) ISBN: 2012 051 084

A fairly detailed 'advanced textbook' approach to the whole subject, with a particular emphasis on Protestantism in France.

Yun, Brother, and Hathaway, P, The Heavenly Man (Monarch Books, London, 2001) ISBN: 1 – 85424 – 597 – X

A terrible and wonderful testimony concerning the extreme persecution of Christians in China. An example of what it means to be a Christian at the start of the 21st Century in those many areas of the world where Christian faith is opposed by the ruling authorities.

Printed in the United States
By Bookmasters